CW01459456

BRANCH LINES AROUND LOWESTOFT

Richard Adderson and Graham Kenworthy

Series editor Vic Mitchell

MP Middleton Press

*Front Cover: Britannia class 4-6-2 no. 70037 **Hereward the Wake** leaves Lowestoft station with an express for Beccles and Liverpool Street during the late 1950s. To the right of the train, the fish loading area is deserted, awaiting Autumn and the start of the herring fishing season. (E.Alger/ ColourRail)*

*Rear Cover: An up express approaches the signal box at the north end of Oulton Broad swing bridge during the late 1950s, hauled by class B17 4-6-0 no. 61631 **Serlby Hall**. The signal post on the left was embedded in the ground at the bottom of the embankment, and was reputedly the tallest in the area. (B.Laughland)*

**Readers of this book may be interested
in the following societies:**

Great Eastern Railway Society
J.R.Tant, Membership Secretary
9 Clare Road
Leytonstone
London E11 1JU

M&GN Circle
G.L.Kenworthy, Membership Secretary
16 Beverley Road
Brundall
Norwich NR13 5QS

Published November 2008

ISBN 978 1 906008 40 6

© Middleton Press, 2008

Design Deborah Esher

Published by
 Middleton Press
 Easebourne Lane
 Midhurst
 West Sussex
 GU29 9AZ
Tel: 01730 813169
Fax: 01730 812601
Email: info@middletonpress.co.uk
www.middletonpress.co.uk

Printed & bound by Biddles Ltd, Kings Lynn

CONTENTS

1.	Yarmouth towards Lowestoft Central	1 – 60
2.	Beccles to Oulton Broad South	61 – 69
3.	Oulton Broad South to Lowestoft South Side	70 – 80
4.	Oulton Broad South to Lowestoft Central	81 – 109
5.	Lowestoft Harbour Works & Harbour	110 – 120

INDEX

66	Barnby		41	Hopton
61	Beccles		99	Lowestoft Central
13	Breydon Viaduct		114	Lowestoft Harbour
8	Caister Road Junction		52	Lowestoft North
57	Coke Ovens Junction		70	Lowestoft South Side
46	Corton		85	Oulton Broad North Junction
37	Gorleston Links Halt		67	Oulton Broad South
27	Gorleston North		1	Yarmouth Beach
29	Gorleston on Sea		22	Yarmouth South Town

ACKNOWLEDGEMENTS

In addition to those individuals acknowledged in the photographic credits, we are most grateful to G.Ashton, C.Fisher, R.Green, N.Langridge, G.Moore, A.Rush and M.Storey-Smith.

Railways of the area in the 1954 showing pre-grouping ownerships. Other maps in this volume are to a scale of 25 ins to 1 mile, with north at the top, unless otherwise stated.

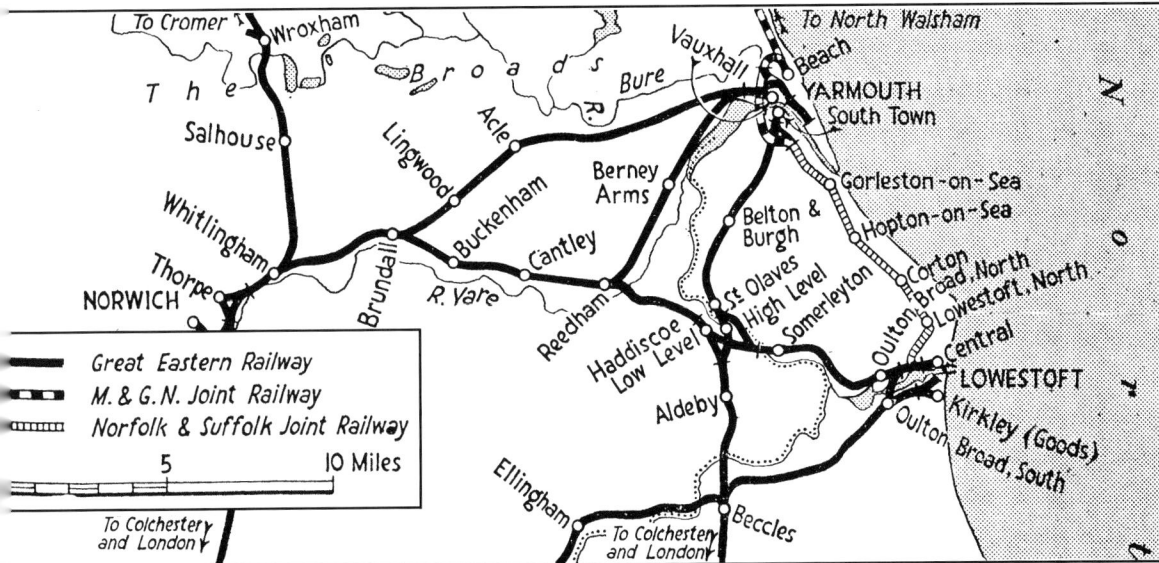

GEOGRAPHICAL SETTING

Yarmouth to Lowestoft

Although starting and finishing virtually at sea level, the route crossed the low plateau of the ancient island of Lothingland. This involved a gradual climb, through cuttings and over embankments, from the Yarmouth end to a summit on the northern fringes of Lowestoft. Apart from taking a westerly route around both towns, slightly further inland, to avoid what were already built-up areas, the line was rarely more than ½ mile from the sea between Gorleston-on-Sea and Lowestoft North stations.

Beccles to Lowestoft

The route is almost level, following the south banks of the River Waveney and Oulton Broad as far as Oulton Broad South and, after crossing Oulton Broad Swing Bridge, the northern edge of Lake Lothing.

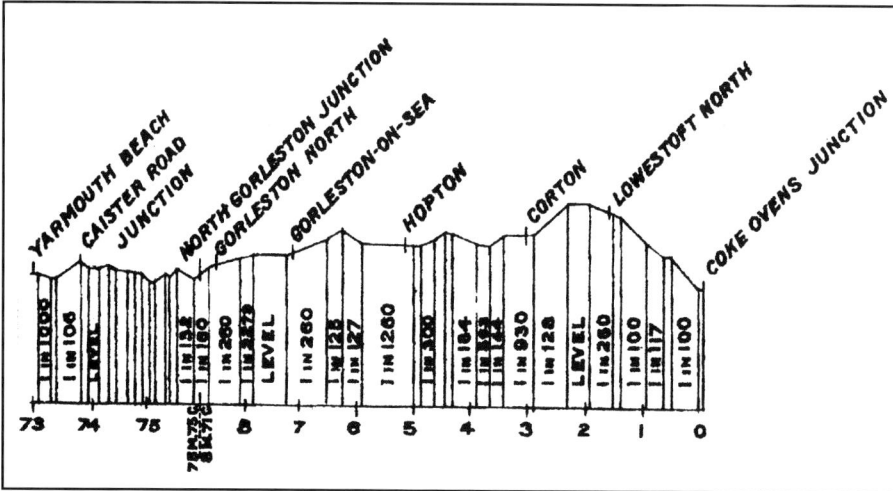

Gradient diagram Yarmouth Beach to Lowestoft.

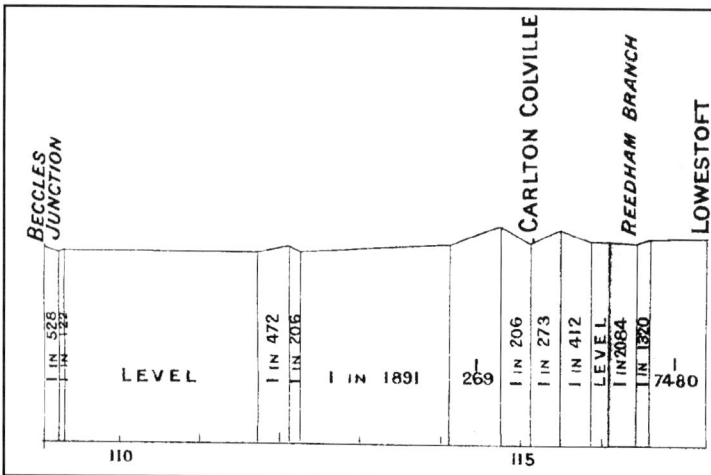

Gradient diagram Beccles to Lowestoft.

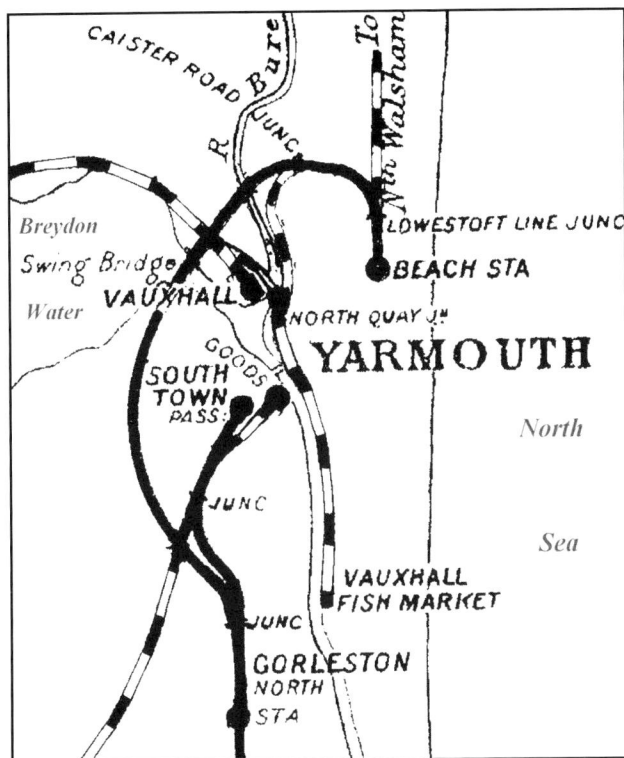

Diagram of Yarmouth railways.

Diagram of Lowestoft railways.

The geography of the two main centres of population featured in this volume is complicated by the presence at both of extensive port facilities and the need for rail links to cross navigable waterways. These enlarged diagrammatic maps of Yarmouth and Lowestoft are included to show the relative locations of the various stations, depots and junctions in these two surprisingly complex towns. Routes described are shown as full lines; those shown dashed are covered in other volumes.

HISTORICAL BACKGROUND

Beccles to Lowestoft Central
(including Oulton Broad South to Lowestoft South Side)

The branch was promoted by the Lowestoft & Beccles Railway Company (L&BR) which was set up in 1855 with the aim of linking the port to the East Suffolk Railway (ESR), hence shortening the route for traffic from Lowestoft to Ipswich and London. The Lowestoft & Beccles Railway Act gained Royal Assent on 23rd June 1856. The line was to have its terminus near St. John's Church in South Lowestoft.

However, while construction was taking place, the East Suffolk Railway (Branch and Capital) Act of 28th June 1858 gave authority for the line to follow an alternative route from a point just east of Carlton Colville station (later Oulton Broad South) via a swing bridge across the western end of Lake Lothing to link up with the route of the Reedham and Lowestoft Railway from Mutford (later Oulton Broad North) to Lowestoft. At first the two routes ran as parallel single lines as far as Coke Ovens Junction before joining for the final few hundred yards to the terminus.

Construction of the originally planned "South Side" line was completed, providing useful freight access to the wharves and businesses located on that side of the harbour, a use which continued for more than a century. In the meantime authority had been sought, and granted, for merger of the L&BR with the ESR under the East Suffolk Railway Companies Amalgamation Act, which gained Royal Assent on 23rd July 1858.

In 1862 the East Suffolk Company joined the Norfolk and Eastern Counties Companies under the Great Eastern Railway umbrella. The Great Eastern Railway passed into the ownership of the London & North Eastern Railway on 1st January 1923, and the lines became part of the Eastern Region of British Railways following nationalisation on 1st January 1948.

The line from Beccles to Lowestoft Central gained added significance when the direct line from the former to Yarmouth South Town closed on 2nd November 1959, with services diverted via Lowestoft. The East Suffolk line survived closure proposals contained in the Beeching Report and went on to become something of a pioneer when it was converted to a system of radio signalling in 1986. Much of the line, including the section through Beccles to Oulton Broad North Junction, was singled as part of this scheme.

On privatisation in 1997, services on the line became part of the Anglia Railways franchise, only to be taken over by **one** Railway in 2004 and rebranded National Express East Anglia in 2008.

Yarmouth to Lowestoft Central

What eventually became the junction towards Lowestoft to the north of Yarmouth Beach was already in place as a result of the opening of the Yarmouth Union Railway by May 1882. This was a combined railway and tramway, designed to connect the recently extended Yarmouth & North Norfolk Railway (later the Midland & Great Northern Joint) to the pre-existing GER tramway, thus providing access to the riverside quays.

At a meeting of the General Managers of the Great Eastern, the Great Northern and the Midland Railways (the last two being those concerned with the local lines of the M&GN Joint Committee) in February 1897, a compromise agreement was reached over the promotion of a coastal line linking the two holiday resorts. The M&GN withdrew their proposed line, except for the portion from Yarmouth Beach to what became North Gorleston Junction while, from the latter to Coke Ovens Junction at Lowestoft, the GER scheme was to be adopted as a joint line between the three companies. A short link between Yarmouth South Town Junction and North Gorleston Junction was owned exclusively by the GER. The M&GN were to have running powers into the GE station at Lowestoft and full access to the harbour and docks.

Although the Act was obtained in 1897, it was another year until Parliamentary approval could be obtained for the setting up of the Norfolk & Suffolk Joint Committee. At the first meeting of the Committee on 2nd November 1898 it was: "Resolved that GER undertake the construction and the maintenance of the proposed new railways between Yarmouth & Lowestoft." The line was opened for traffic on 13th July 1903.

Following the 1923 Grouping the M&GN and the N&S Joint Committees continued to exist because their parent companies had been divided between the London & North Eastern and London, Midland & Scottish Railways. This situation was simplified in October 1936 following an agreement by the LNER and LMSR that administration of both Joint Committees' lines should pass to the LNER with the LMSR keeping a watching brief on policy matters.

The lines became part of the Eastern Region of British Railways upon nationalisation on 1st January 1948. Closure of the link from Yarmouth Beach to North Gorleston Junction took place on 21st September 1953.

Following closure of the direct East Suffolk Line route from Beccles to Yarmouth South Town in November 1959, the branch took on a new lease of life, with trains diverted via Lowestoft. The increased activity was short-lived as, following the Beeching Report of 1963, a general rationalisation followed with singling of the line taking place in November 1967. Closure followed on 2nd May 1970.

PASSENGER SERVICES

Yarmouth to Lowestoft

Although it is acknowledged that, for most of the line's existence, the three months of Summer traffic was much heavier than that of the remainder of the year, the purpose of this brief account is to demonstrate the development and decline of the day to day services provided.

The very first timetable in July 1903 indicated the level of Summer traffic anticipated with four GER trains originating from Yarmouth South Town to Lowestoft Central, together with eight M&GN services from Beach Station; however, four of this latter total terminated at Lowestoft North.

For the most part, there was more or less equal provision from both companies, exemplified by the 1912/3 Winter timetable. The GER ran four trains from Yarmouth South Town, with the M&GN contributing five from Beach station.

Due to wartime economies all GER trains were withdrawn between Yarmouth South Town and Lowestoft Central as from the January 1917 timetable, the service being reinstated for the post-war Summer traffic in July 1919.

The level of service by the late 1930s is illustrated by the 1937/8 timetable which detailed eight trains from South Town and six from Beach which ran each weekday, the vast majority calling at all stations.

During World War II space for wagon storage was required and it was a relatively easy matter to close one line and introduce single line working. This was done between Gorleston on Sea and Lowestoft North, commencing early in June 1942; normal operation was not restored until March 1948.

In the post-war timetable of 1945/6 there were, unsurprisingly, fewer trains than at any earlier date. Only four ran from South Town and a meagre two from Beach. However these called at all stations, with the exception of Gorleston North, which had closed in October 1942 following bomb damage in the previous February.

After closure of the line from Beach station to North Gorleston Junction in 1953 and the introduction of DMUs, the Winter service of 1957/8 showed 15 hourly departures from South Town from 7.29 am to 9.29 pm. This rose to 20 in 1963/4 after closure of the direct line to Beccles, but, by the final winter of 1969/70, the number had fallen to 12.

Beccles to Lowestoft

For just over a century, this line acted as a connecting branch from and to the main East Suffolk line between Ipswich and Yarmouth South Town. In January 1853 there were eight trains, the majority of which connected with main line services.

Sixty years later, in 1912/3, this had risen only marginally to ten, despite the doubling of the line from Beccles to Oulton Broad North Junction.

By the Winter of 1937/8 there were 15 daily services and, although there was a marked reduction during the subsequent war years, numbers rose again to 11 during 1945/6.
1963/4 saw a total of 18 trains, two of which worked through from London, the remaining 16 from either Ipswich or Halesworth.

By 1986, the year that radio signalling was commissioned, there were nine trains, all originating from Ipswich; but by 2008, even though the number had only increased to ten, seven of them were through services from Liverpool Street

1. Yarmouth towards Lowestoft Central

YARMOUTH BEACH

I.   This 1928 plan shows the station layout at its most extensive, many of the additions being due to the opening of the line to Lowestoft via Breydon Bridge in 1903.

1.   Lowestoft line trains tended to use the western platform, which had been added in 1903, coinciding with the opening of the new line. Class C12 4-4-2T no. 4015 is waiting here on 17th June 1938, and soon it will be heading out over Breydon Water with the early afternoon train for Lowestoft. Passengers have the choice of travelling in either a 6-wheel coach, or a former LNWR bogie vehicle. (M.Yarwood/GW Trust coll.)

2.   The station was a terminus, so all trains between the main line and the Lowestoft line needed to reverse before continuing their journey. Whilst this was a straightforward procedure for passenger trains, through freight workings added to the general activity in the goods yard, where 0-6-0T no. 093 is busy shunting a long line of wagons, again in June 1938. (M.Yarwood/GW Trust coll.)

3.   Locomotives from the GER network could easily make their way here while the Lowestoft line remained in use, and a class J50 0-6-0T, still carrying its LNER number 8924, was one such visitor on Easter Sunday 1950. This engine was normally used on carriage shunting at Norwich Thorpe, and the shunting pole on the front suggests it would be used on equally mundane duties during its stay at the seaside. After the Lowestoft line closed, the variety of motive power seen at Beach station decreased dramatically - although there were convoluted connections through the streets of Yarmouth and at North Walsham, the nearest direct access to the rest of the system was then 40 miles away at Melton Constable. (K.G.Leighton)

4.   There is a distinctly Great Eastern flavour to the motive power as class D16/3 4-4-0 no. 62561 arrives with a train from Derby to Lowestoft on 14th July 1951, passing two class B12/3 4-6-0s standing in the shed yard.
(B.W.L Brooksbank/Initial Photographics)

Other views of this station can be found in our earlier volume *Melton Constable to Yarmouth Beach*.

5.   Once the train had come to a stand, class F4 2-4-2T no. 67176 backed on to the LMSR coaches for the last leg of the journey. This heavy load was quite a task for the little tank engine, and a plume of smoke at the back of the train shows that 62561 is providing a welcome push out of the platform. With the steep curving climb from Nelson Road to come, the driver and fireman of the F4 were no doubt very grateful for this assistance. (B.W.L Brooksbank/Initial Photographics)

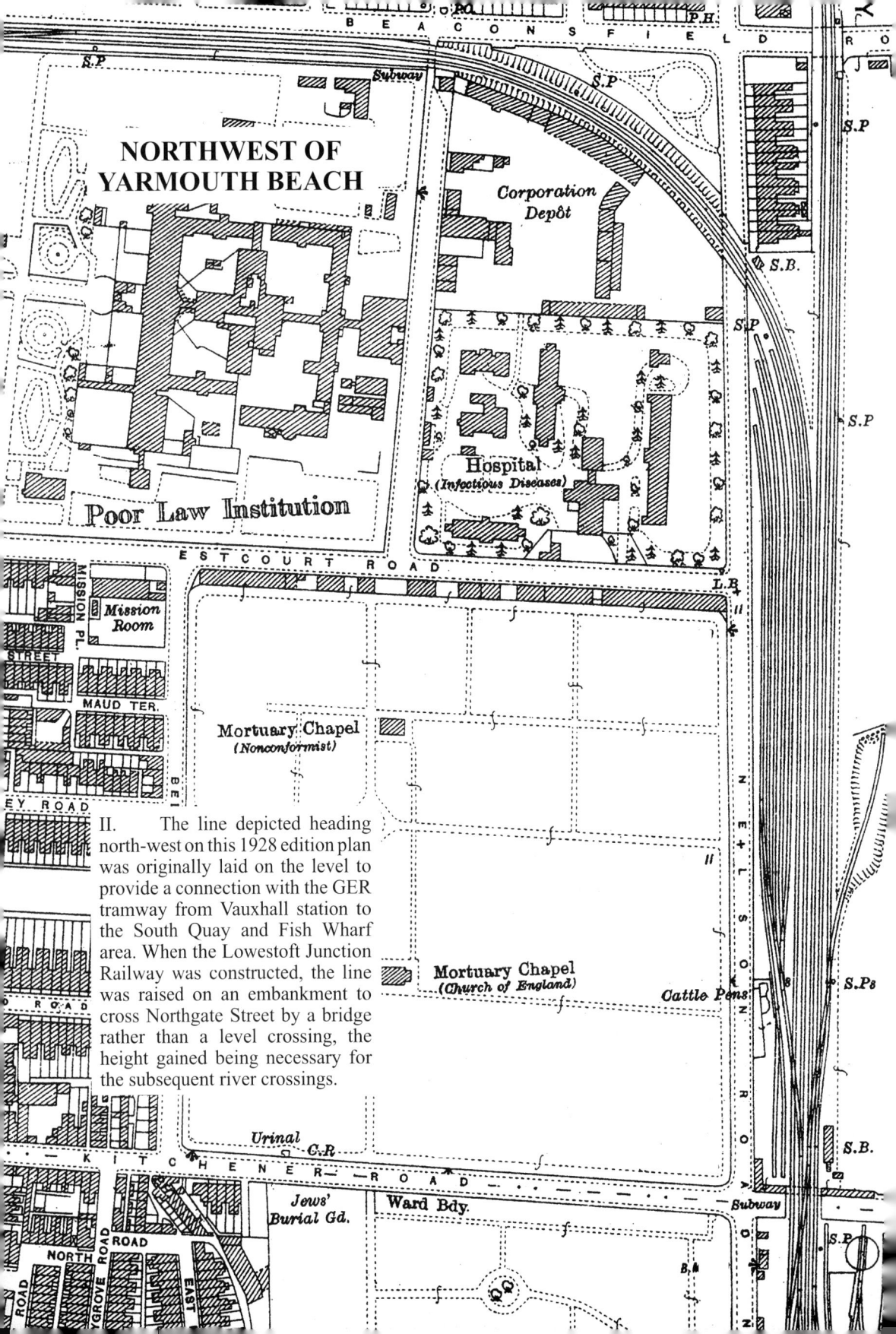

NORTHWEST OF YARMOUTH BEACH

S.P

BEACONSFIELD R O

P.H

Subway

S.P

S.P

Corporation Depôt

S.B.

S.P

S.P

Hospital
(Infectious Diseases)

Poor Law Institution

L.B

E S T C O U R T R O A D

MISSION PL.

Mission Room

STREET

MAUD TER.

BE

Mortuary Chapel
(Nonconformist)

EY ROAD

II.　　The line depicted heading north-west on this 1928 edition plan was originally laid on the level to provide a connection with the GER tramway from Vauxhall station to the South Quay and Fish Wharf area. When the Lowestoft Junction Railway was constructed, the line was raised on an embankment to cross Northgate Street by a bridge rather than a level crossing, the height gained being necessary for the subsequent river crossings.

Mortuary Chapel
(Church of England)

Cattle Pens

S.Ps

ROAD

Urinal
C.R

S.B.

K I T C H E N E R R O A D

Jews'
Burial Gd.

Ward Bdy.

Subway

ROAD

NORTH

GROVE ROAD

EAST

B.M

S.P

6.   Leaving Beach station, the Lowestoft line ran parallel with the main line for a short distance, before heading westwards to cross Nelson Road on the level. The signal box by the level crossing, seen here on 11th February 1959, marked the start of a heavily engineered section of railway to North Gorleston Junction, and, to a slightly lesser degree, on to Lowestoft. It was a great contrast with most other lines in the area, which tended to merge unobtrusively into the landscape. The construction costs were enormous and, although the line allowed the M&GN access to the thriving fishing port of Lowestoft, it had a working life of only 50 years. (J.Bull)

7.   Climbing away from Nelson Road on a gradient of 1 in 106, the railway was carried on an embankment supported by massive concrete retaining walls, faced with blue bricks. We are looking westwards towards Caister Road Junction in the early 1960s. During the demolition work, the earth had been excavated from between the walls, clearly revealing the method of construction. One of the walls was still standing in 2008, providing the only major reminder of the railway in this vicinity. (B.Reading)

CAISTER ROAD JUNCTION TOWARDS BREYDON VIADUCT

III. Caister Road Junction marks the divergence of the 1903 route to Lowestoft from the 1882 Yarmouth Union line which headed due south towards the riverside quays; the signal box appears at the eastern edge of this 1928 plan. The route continues in a southwesterly direction skirting the western side of the town, crossing pre-existing features on a series of bridges. In this and the following section we will deal with these in geographical order as the line passes over Lawn Avenue, the River Bure, the Norwich to Yarmouth main road, the Norwich to Yarmouth Vauxhall railway and, most impressively, Breydon Water.

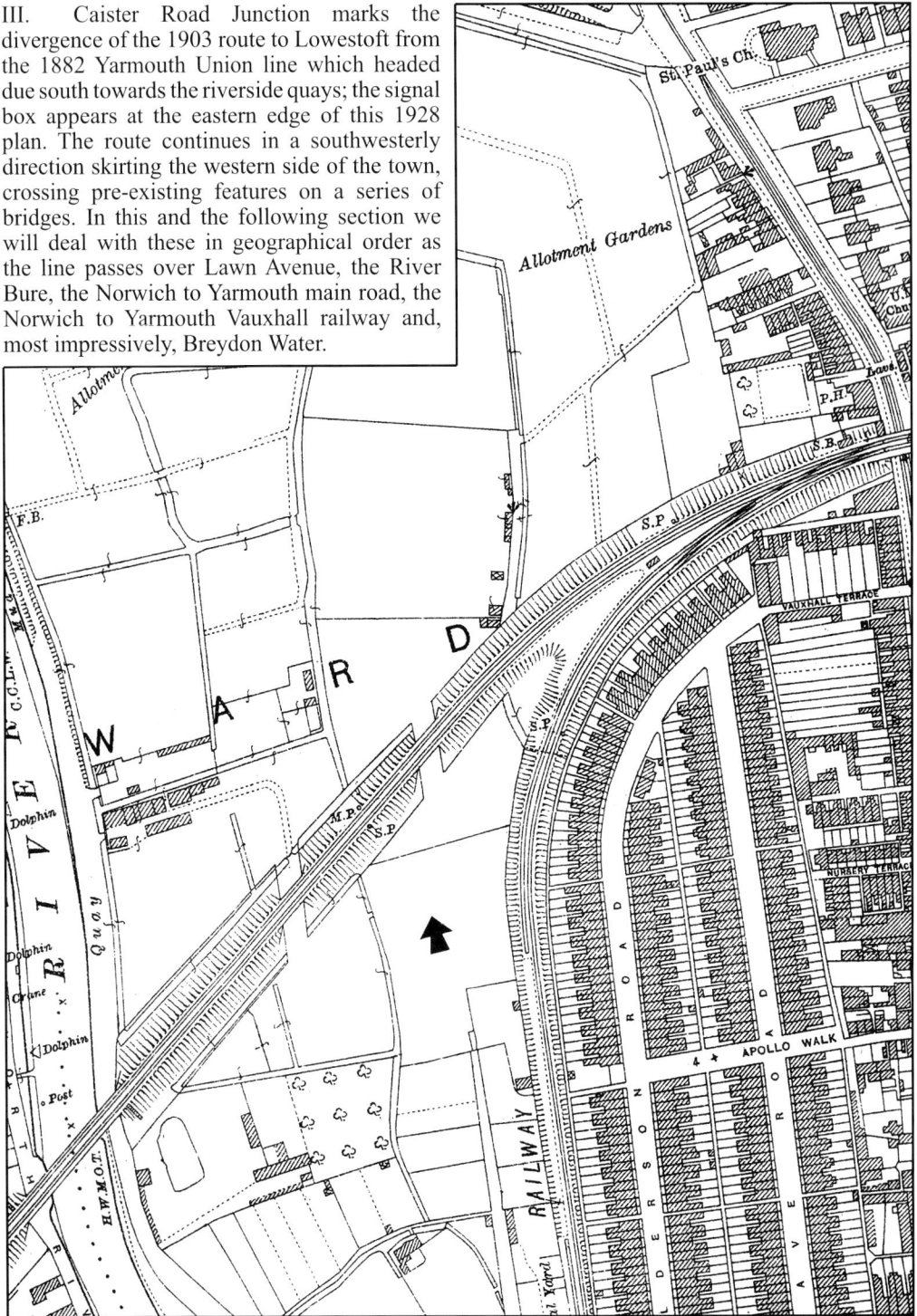

IV.   This continuation of the plan shows the line crossing the A47 main road and Vauxhall station approach before crossing the eastern edge of Breydon Water. If a similar map was produced in 2008, the Yarmouth Western Bypass would be shown following exactly the same alignment.

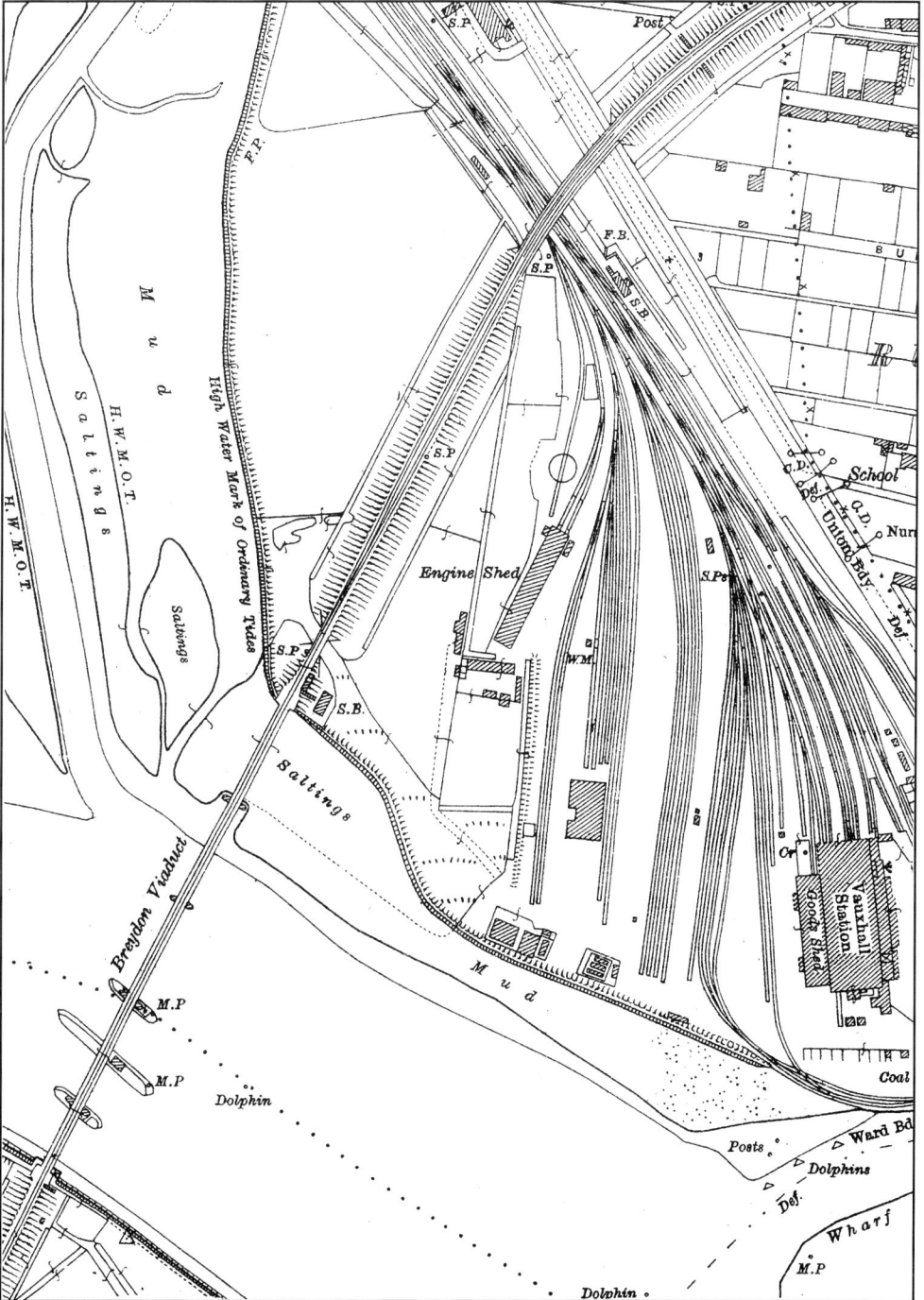

8.   At Caister Road Junction, the line to White Swan coal yard swung away to the south, following the alignment of the original ground level line towards the docks. The rusty and overgrown state of the main line dates this picture between closure in September 1953 and June 1954, when the signal box was abolished. By contrast the branch to White Swan yard is shiny, and two goods trains a day were booked to work over this line until the closure of Beach station on 28th February 1959. (R.J.Adderson coll.)

9. South westwards from Caister Road Junction, the abandoned line rusted away gently through the 1950s, although the section south of Breydon bridge saw occasional use for wagon storage. Total closure of the M&GN main line eliminated any lingering possibility that services might be restored, and work on lifting the track began only a few days after this sad event. A rather battered looking steam crane is engaged on this task during the Spring of 1959, with the girders of Lawn Avenue bridge in the foreground. (Archant Norwich)

10. Now we are looking northwards along a traffic-free Lawn Avenue, towards the railway bridge, on 8th April 1960. A traditional road sign warns large vehicles of the restricted height of the bridge, but gives them very little time in which to stop. (J.Bull)

11. The next obstacle to the railway was the River Bure, which was crossed by a substantial girder bridge. Here is the bridge, seen from the north on 8th April 1960, with smaller spans crossing minor roads on either side of the river. This structure survived the wholesale demolitions of 1959/60 as it carried utility pipes and cables, and was eventually dismantled in February 1977. (J.Bull)

12.   Next came the viaduct carrying the line over the main A47 road and the approaches to Yarmouth Vauxhall station, the terminus of the GER route from Norwich. This was the scene on 28th June 1959, with the signal box at Vauxhall station prominent. The embankment to the extreme left of the picture, formerly the approach to Breydon viaduct, has already been removed, and the earth used as infill for new carriage sidings at the former GER station. Once demolition work started, the gangs made rapid progress - the girders spanning the railway were removed in August 1959, and those over the road came down in December. However the brick piers remained for some years afterwards, providing a rather untidy welcome for visitors to the town. (J.Dean)

BREYDON VIADUCT

13.   Construction of the viaduct began in 1899, and here we see a very early stage in the work, with the piers beginning to take shape. The GER locomotive shed is a prominent feature over on the north bank of Breydon Water. (G.L.Kenworthy coll.)

14.   Here is the viaduct in all its splendour, shortly after completion. The three northerly spans and the swing span were identical in size – 169' 10" long and 24' 2" in depth, whilst the span at the Lowestoft end, was shorter (110' 6") and shallower (17'), but of similar general appearance to the others. A structure of this size in what had been remote marshland caused something of a sensation in the neighbourhood, prompting the *Eastern Daily Press* to refer to it in July 1903 as "the local Tay bridge" – a somewhat unfortunate analogy in view of events less than 25 years earlier! (G.L.Kenworthy coll.)

15.   The bridge was controlled from a cabin known as the turret, situated on top of the swinging span. From here the bridgeman had an elevated view over the waterways, giving him plenty of warning of approaching shipping. This is the inside of the turret in the early days, full of gleaming machinery powered by a gas engine. It took about four minutes to swing the bridge, from the moment that the locking bolts were withdrawn to the time that the span was brought to a stand at right angles to the railway. At times the river traffic was heavy, and it is reported that a train was delayed one day in 1904 while no fewer than 17 boats went through the bridge.
(G.L.Kenworthy coll.)

➜   16. Not only was the line expensive to build, but it was far from cheap to operate, especially in view of the somewhat sparse train service. It was double track throughout, except for the section over Breydon Water, and, as we can see from this picture, dated 26th September 1911, there was originally a signal box at each end of the viaduct. This extravagance lasted for a quarter of a century, but in 1928 the arrangements were modified so that the signalman at Caister Road Junction signal box controlled all movements over the bridge. At a lower level, the GER loco shed, turntable and coaling stage complete the picture. (GERS/Windwood Collection)

17.   The photographer has ventured almost up to the girders to obtain this picture of a class J17 0-6-0 crossing the viaduct with a passenger train from Lowestoft, just a few years before closure. (B.Reading)

18. A former GER 2-4-2T → emerges from the bridge onto the south bank of Breydon Water on 8th April 1950. The mound in the field is the site of a somewhat remote dock and which was home to the pleasure steamer *Waterfly* from 1894 until the mid-1930s. (K.G.Leighton)

19. The bridge remained in place for some nine years after the last train ran, a challenge to navigation and frequented only by seabirds and adventurous local urchins. Riding high in the water after unloading further up the Yare, the MV *Festivity* negotiates the swinging span, now permanently open to river traffic, on 1st October 1955. This was one of the F.T Everard fleet of coasters, which were regular visitors to these waters for many years. (P.J.Kelley)

→ 20. We take a final look at the disappearing central span during the Spring of 1962. The inevitable task of demolition had begun in March 1962, and by the end of the month the two northern spans, over dry land and tidal mud, had been toppled over and cut up where they lay. By contrast, this third span was a more difficult proposition, being over deep water. Piles were driven to support the structure whilst it was being demolished, and the contractor employed an 80ft. crane, mounted on a pontoon, to load the scrap metal into lighters. Once the spans had been cut up, the brick piers were destroyed by explosives, and by June, the great bridge was but a memory, except for a few sections of the decking which were used in roof repair work at Norwich Thorpe station. (G.L.Kenworthy coll.)

NORTH GORLESTON
JUNCTION

North Gorleston Junction

Posts

Posts

Sl.

G.P

F.B

Marsh House

Timber Yard

Saw Mills

S.B.

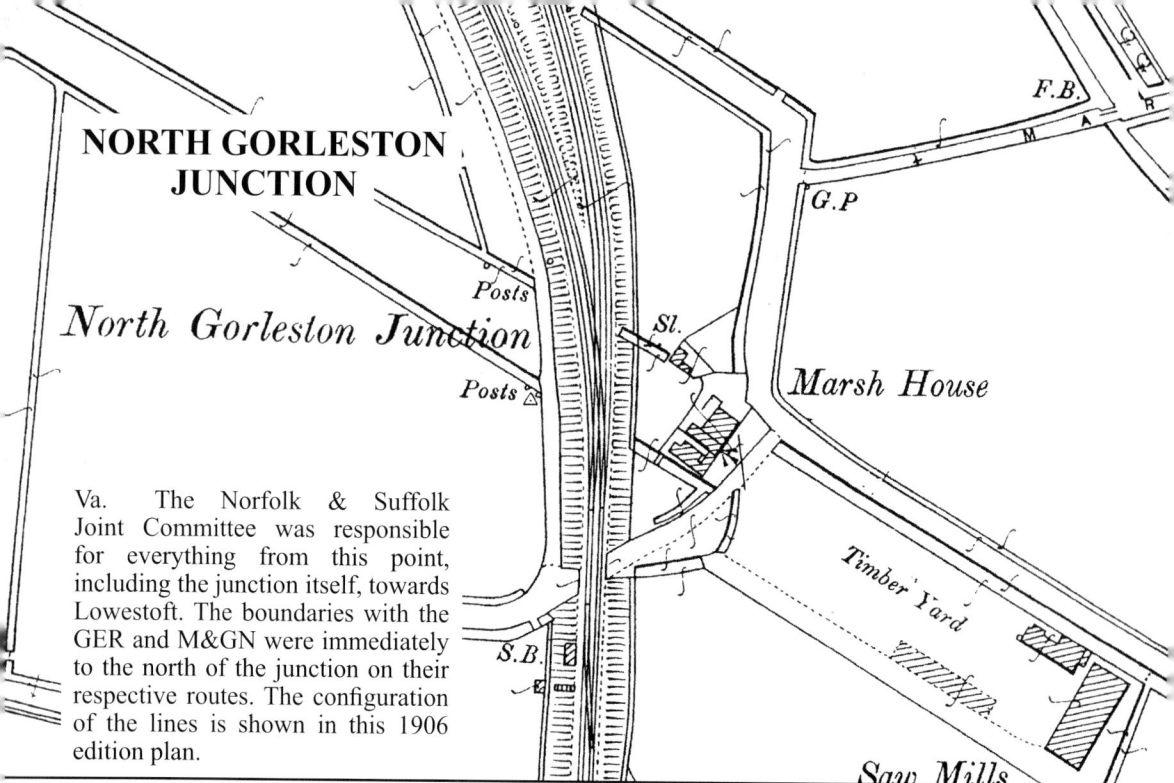

Va. The Norfolk & Suffolk Joint Committee was responsible for everything from this point, including the junction itself, towards Lowestoft. The boundaries with the GER and M&GN were immediately to the north of the junction on their respective routes. The configuration of the lines is shown in this 1906 edition plan.

21.   After crossing further bridges over roads, minor waterways, and finally the tracks of the GER route from Yarmouth South Town to Beccles, the M&GN joined the GER at the remote North Gorleston Junction. This is the junction, looking in a generally northward direction on 11th October 1911, with the town of Great Yarmouth visible in the distance across the open fields. The signal box was switched out when the line from Beach station closed, and was abolished on 11th October 1955. In later years, all traces of the railway here disappeared under a sprawling industrial estate. (GERS/Windwood Collection)

YARMOUTH SOUTH TOWN

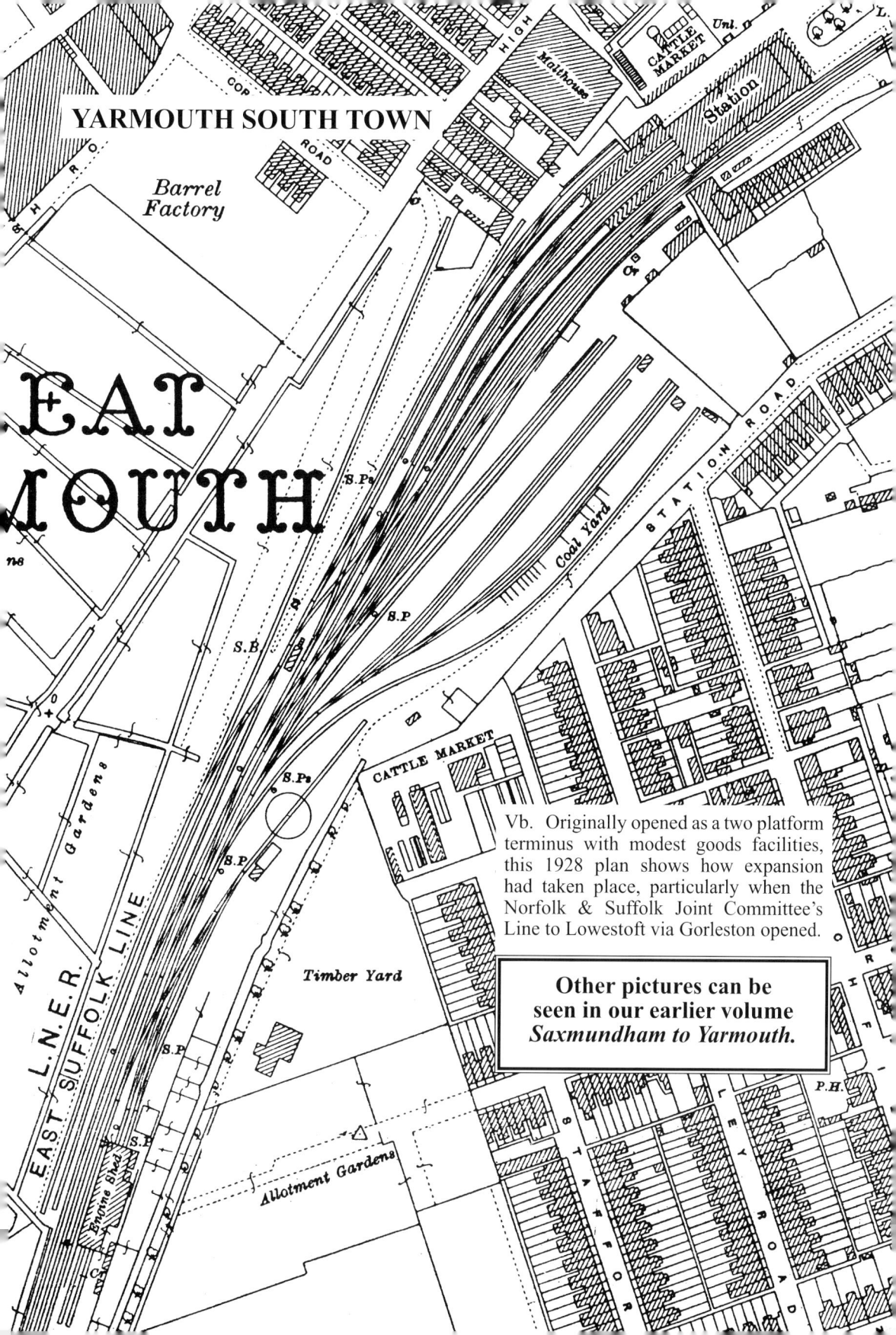

Barrel Factory

EAT MOUTH

CATTLE MARKET

Station

Maltings

Barrel Factory

Coal Yard

STATION ROAD

S.P

S.B.

Allotment Gardens

EAST SUFFOLK LINE

L.N.E.R.

Engine Shed

Timber Yard

Allotment Gardens

CATTLE MARKET

P.H.

Vb. Originally opened as a two platform terminus with modest goods facilities, this 1928 plan shows how expansion had taken place, particularly when the Norfolk & Suffolk Joint Committee's Line to Lowestoft via Gorleston opened.

Other pictures can be seen in our earlier volume *Saxmundham to Yarmouth*.

22.   This view looking eastwards across the station area on 26th September 1911 vividly illustrates the extent of the land occupied by the railway. Rakes of coaches stand at the platforms of the passenger station, an almost insignificant feature to the left of the picture, while a tank engine is shunting in the busy goods yard. Coal and timber traffic is particularly evident here. The clock tower of the Town Hall can be seen on the skyline across the river, while a number of factory chimneys show the scale of the industry to be found around the harbour. (GERS/Windwood Collection)

23.   A Brush Type 2 diesel waits to leave with an express on 6th April 1962. It will take the coastal route to Lowestoft, where the train will reverse before continuing its journey to Liverpool Street. The neat platforms and modern electric lights are the result of major improvement works at the station, which had been completed only eight years previously. (R.J.Adderson collection)

24.   The final passenger trains were the 20.19 from Lowestoft and 21.10 back from Yarmouth on 2nd May 1970. In order to cater for the "last day" crowds, the usual railcar was coupled to two similar units for this round trip. Carrying a headboard to mark the occasion, the train waits to leave South Town for the last time. (R.J.Adderson)

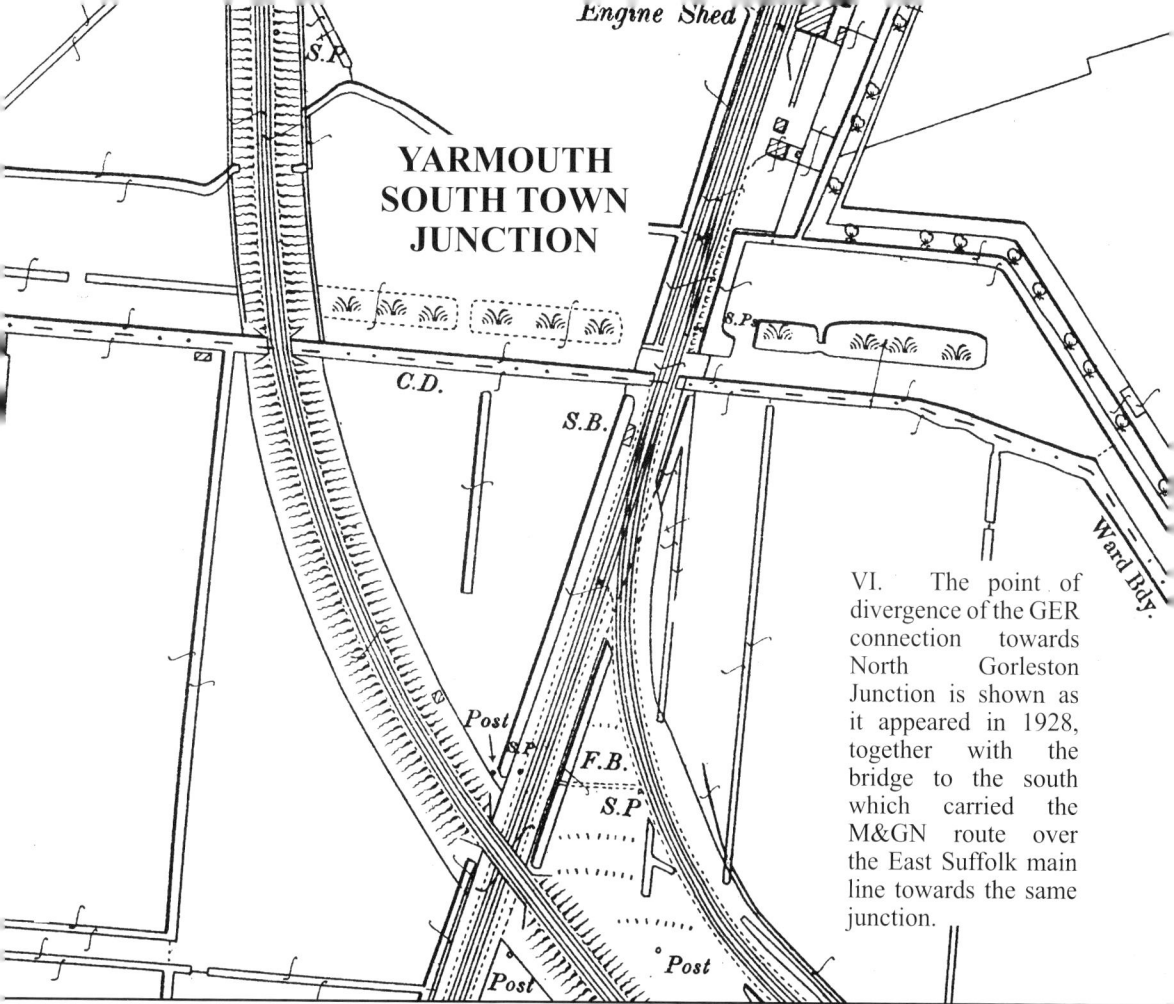

YARMOUTH SOUTH TOWN JUNCTION

Engine Shed

S.P.

C.D.

S.B.

S.P.

Post

S.P.

F.B.

S.P.

Post

Post

Post

Ward Bdy.

VI. The point of divergence of the GER connection towards North Gorleston Junction is shown as it appeared in 1928, together with the bridge to the south which carried the M&GN route over the East Suffolk main line towards the same junction.

25. We are looking in a south-westerly direction from the up starter signal in 1911, with a GER 4-4-0 standing in the locomotive shed yard. Beyond South Town Junction signal box, the distant bridge and embankment carry the M&GN line, while the tracks diverging to the left curve round to make the connection at North Gorleston Junction. (GERS/Windwood Collection)

26. After years of hosting a purely local day-to-day service, the line through Gorleston found itself handling long distance and express trains from January 1959, with the introduction of through trains to Beccles, Ipswich and London. This proved to be the beginning of the process leading to closure of the direct line between Yarmouth and Beccles in November. With the M&GN bridge to the left, class B17 4-6-0 no. 61664 *Liverpool* heads towards North Gorleston Junction with a train from South Town to Liverpool Street on 19th April 1959. (I.C.Allen/Transport Treasury)

(18—V19)

MIDLAND & GREAT NORTHERN RAILWAYS JOINT COMMITTEE.

TO

GORLESTON NORTH.

Via YARMOUTH BEACH & N. & S. JOINT.

Norfolk & Suffo— —oint Rys. Com.
Not tr— —sferable.

GORLESTON NORTH to
GORLESTON NORTH   GORLESTON NORTH

NOTTINGHAM MID.
NOTTINGHAM MID   NOTTINGHAM MID
Via Bourne & Saxby

FARE 11/0 THIRD CLASS FARE 11/0
SEE CONDITIONS ON BACK

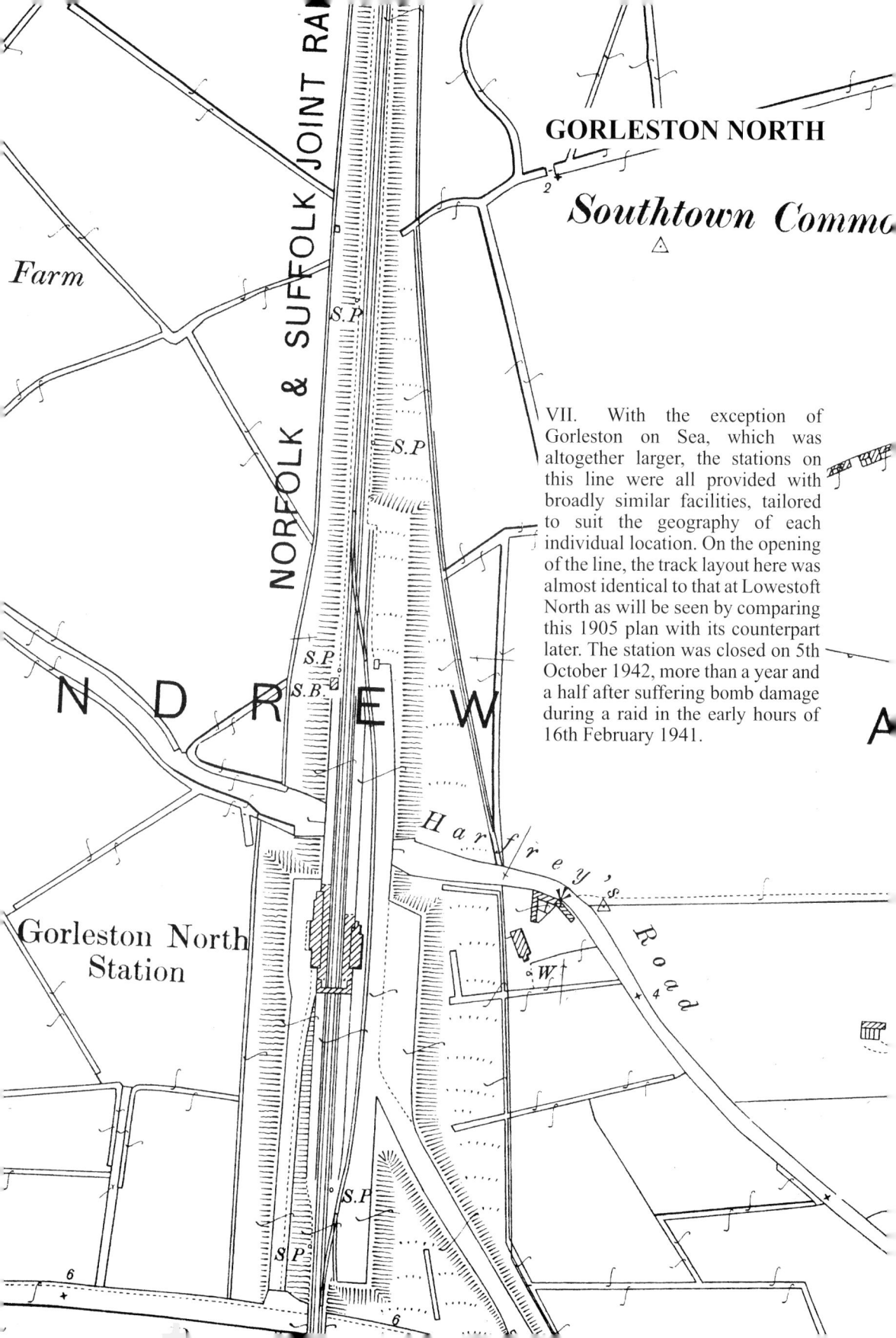

GORLESTON NORTH

Southtown Commo

NORFOLK & SUFFOLK JOINT RA

Farm

S.P

S.P

S.P
S.B

N D R E W

VII. With the exception of Gorleston on Sea, which was altogether larger, the stations on this line were all provided with broadly similar facilities, tailored to suit the geography of each individual location. On the opening of the line, the track layout here was almost identical to that at Lowestoft North as will be seen by comparing this 1905 plan with its counterpart later. The station was closed on 5th October 1942, more than a year and a half after suffering bomb damage during a raid in the early hours of 16th February 1941.

A

Harfrey's Road

W

Gorleston North
Station

S.P

S.P

27.   The platforms here were supported on brick arches, giving extra support for the elevated construction. Once the embankment had been built up around them, this feature was not immediately apparent, but the tops of the arches were visible in the brickwork of the platform face. As we shall see later, Hopton station was constructed in a similar fashion. This is the view southwards soon after the line was opened. (M&GN Trust)

28.   Now we are standing at track level, looking towards the station on 11th October 1911, with a GER shunt signal on the right controlling the southern entrance to the goods siding. Spanning this, the twin arms of the loading gauge reflect the slight, but potentially critical, differences between the clearances permitted on the GER and M&GN systems. The goods "yard" consisted of little more than a loop behind the platform. However, the embankment widened considerably here, forming an artificial plateau, which allowed plenty of scope for possible future expansion. As it turned out, this space was never needed. (GERS/Windwood Collection)

GORLESTON ON SEA

VIII. This 1906 plan, surveyed shortly after the opening of the line, gives an indication of the high expectations for the town's development as a fashionable seaside resort. A large area of land to the west of the line was purchased in anticipation of expanded station facilities as demand grew. In the event the original installation proved to be adequate for the traffic generated, and much of the spare land was subsequently sold off.

NILE ROAD

Reservoir

Yarmouth 3
Lowestoft 6
M.S

S.Ps

F.B.

Station Hotel

W.M.

Goods Shed

Gorleston-on-Sea
Station

AVONDALE ROAD

CLARENCE ROAD

S.P.

Cr.

S.B.

← 29. This was the view northwards along the platform in the very early days, with the covered footbridge beyond the buildings. The Station Hotel is taking shape to the left of the picture – no doubt the owners were anticipating worthwhile trade from the coming of the railway. (M&GN Trust)

← 30. Now we are looking south from the footbridge with Intermediate class 2-4-0 no. 496 heading a passenger train. This picture also dates from the very early days, and was used to illustrate the 1903 *Railway Magazine* article describing the opening of the line. The long covered passageways provide access to the platforms from the road level booking office. (M&GN Trust)

31. Here is the signalman's view of the station and yard some eight years later, on 11th October 1911, with the spacious goods yard doing a good trade in coal and other traffic. This was the only station on the line to be provided with a goods shed, and a substantial one it was too, measuring 85ft. by 35ft. The 5-ton crane is also shown in the picture. (GERS/Windwood Collection)

← 32. The booking office at road level, seen here at Christmas 1962, was a fairly simple structure, giving little clue to the impressive range of buildings to be found on each platform. From here a pathway led directly down to the northbound platform, whilst a footbridge crossed the tracks, leading to the ramp giving access to the opposite platform. By now the paths to the platforms were open to the elements, the walls and roofs seen in picture 30 having long since vanished. These arrangements were superseded soon afterwards, when a new booking office was installed in the under-used station buildings. (J. Dean)

← 33. No D5527 pulls into the station with an up express, around 1960. This was during the line's brief "main line" period, when the trains between Yarmouth South Town and Liverpool Street travelled this way following the closure of the line between Yarmouth and Beccles. The ten coaches are a random mixture of Gresley, Thompson and British Railways designs, a formation typical of the time. (B.Reading)

34.   There is still double track and a crossover on 27th February 1967, but by now the station is no longer staffed, and vegetation is taking hold on the platforms. The footbridge is a recent addition, having been erected here when the booking office was relocated. This much-travelled structure had seen previous use at Whitwell & Reepham and Roughton Road Junction, but it would not last much longer, as it was cut up after the line was singled. (Railway Record of the British Isles/G.L.Pring)

35.   All the stations became unstaffed with effect from 12th September 1966, and "One Train Working" over a single line was introduced from November 1967; in effect, after that date, the line was operated as a long siding from the Lowestoft end. By the last day of services, an air of neglect was all too apparent - the economies may have reduced the running costs, but had done nothing to encourage potential travellers. A Cravens DMU pauses briefly in the shadow of the boarded-up and crumbling buildings, before continuing its journey to Lowestoft. (R.J.Adderson)

36.   The station buildings were demolished in February 1976 following persistent vandalism, and fifteen years later the derelict site was swallowed up by a new road scheme, utilising the course of the railway from just south of the station to North Gorleston Junction. In September 1991, the cutting to the north of the distant Station Road bridge is still recognisable as a former railway, but the contractors have started their work. Very soon, this stretch of line would become a busy and charmless stretch of dual carriageway. (S.McNae)

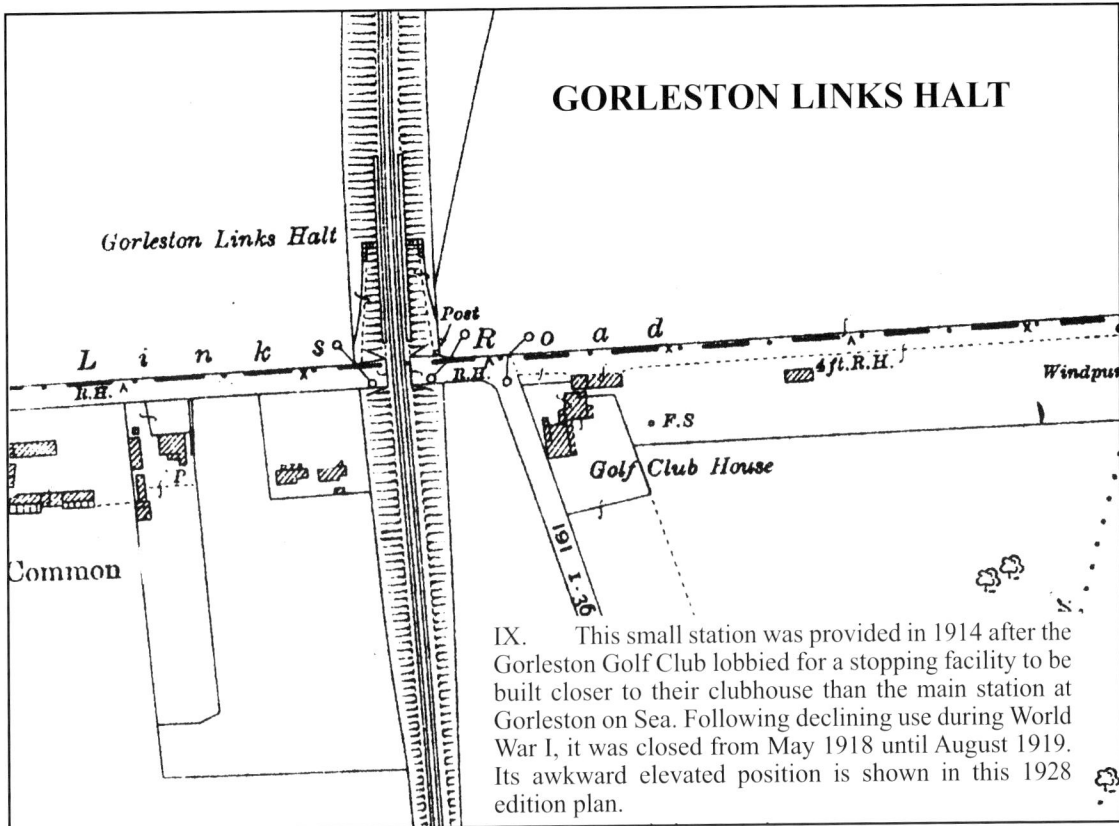

GORLESTON LINKS HALT

Gorleston Links Halt

Common

IX.   This small station was provided in 1914 after the Gorleston Golf Club lobbied for a stopping facility to be built closer to their clubhouse than the main station at Gorleston on Sea. Following declining use during World War I, it was closed from May 1918 until August 1919. Its awkward elevated position is shown in this 1928 edition plan.

37.   The halt itself consisted of two short concrete platforms, totally devoid of any facilities for the passengers, in an exposed position perched on top of an embankment. This basic structure is apparent as class D16/3 4-4-0 no. 62570 passes with the 10.50 a.m. "Holiday Camps Express" from Gorleston to Liverpool Street on 31st August 1957. (B.Harrison)

← 38. Access to each of the platforms was identical, with a rough path climbing gradually from the road, followed by a steep flight of steps up to rail level. The sign confirms that this is the approach to the platform serving northbound trains on 27th February 1967. (Railway Record of the British Isles/G.L.Pring)

← 39. During the 1960s there was considerable housing development to the east, between the railway and the sea. However, it came too late to generate any appreciable traffic for the railway, and it was left to Great Yarmouth Corporation buses to provide transport for the residents. This picture, taken on 2nd May 1970, sums it all up. (G.H.Smith)

40. We take a last look at the halt, as a railcar heads for Yarmouth on the last day. After closure, the embankment was flattened to make way for more housing, and all trace of the railway here quickly vanished. (R.J.Adderson)

HOPTON

41.   Here we have another picture from the early optimistic days of the line, with the promoters' ambitions once more illustrated by the range of buildings and lengthy platforms. Looking southwards, there is a remarkable similarity to the contemporary scene at Gorleston North shown in picture 27. (M&GN Trust)

X.   With the designed absence of public level crossings on the branch, unusual for East Anglia, this station was one of those constructed on an embankment. This 1927 edition indicates the lofty position here with the sloping approach roads to the goods yard and to the main station building.

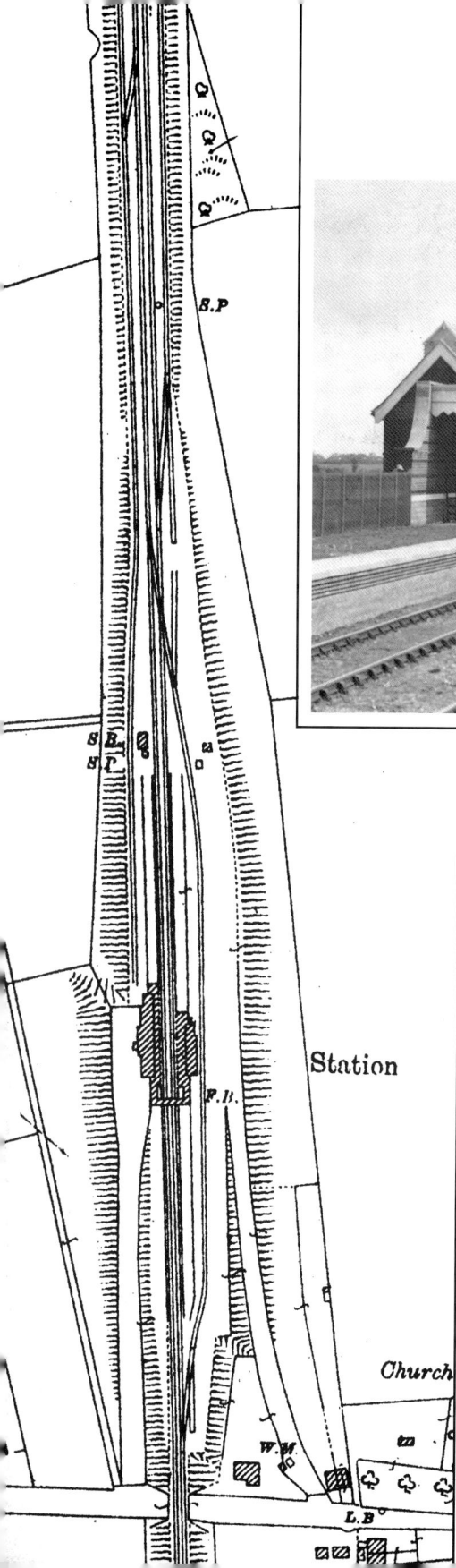

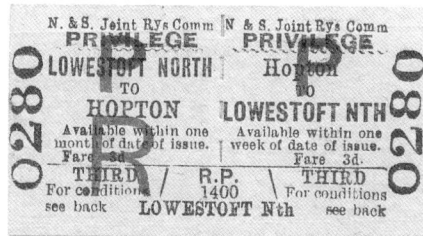

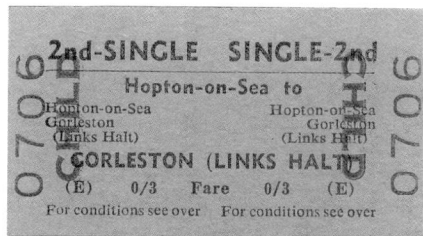

42.   Some 50 years later, the spacious layout is still apparent, but by now it has become obvious that the anticipated development and associated traffic will never happen. Class J17 0-6-0 no. 65507 does a little shunting before setting off northwards with a pick-up goods train in 1954. The goods yard closed in July 1964, and the signal box was abolished some six months later. (R.E.Vincent/Transport Treasury)

43.   On the same day, class F5 2-4-2T no. 67218 propels a two-coach pull-push train towards Lowestoft. Each platform was supported on a row of 38 brick arches, which were revealed briefly when the station was demolished and the site levelled in 1981 - the discovery of something resembling an ancient aqueduct was the cause of some comment locally at the time. We can see the top of one of these arches at the base of the platform on the extreme left of the picture. (R.E.Vincent/Transport Treasury)

44.   Camping coaches were first recorded here, and at Corton and Lowestoft North, in 1935, and following an inevitable break during the war, the facility was restored in 1952. In view of the amount of space available in the goods yard, it is somewhat surprising that a length of track was laid on the platform in order to accommodate these vehicles. Here we see Pullman Camping Coaches CC168 and CC169, formerly named *Palmyra* and *Grosvenor* respectively, on 4th February 1967. They were out of use by this time, and were cut up on site soon afterwards. (J.Watling)

45.   The main platform buildings were typical of the GER architectural style of the time and the basic design was repeated at the other intermediate stations along the line. This is the exterior of the building on the western platform on 27th February 1967.
(Railway Record of the British Isles/G.L.Pring)

CORTON

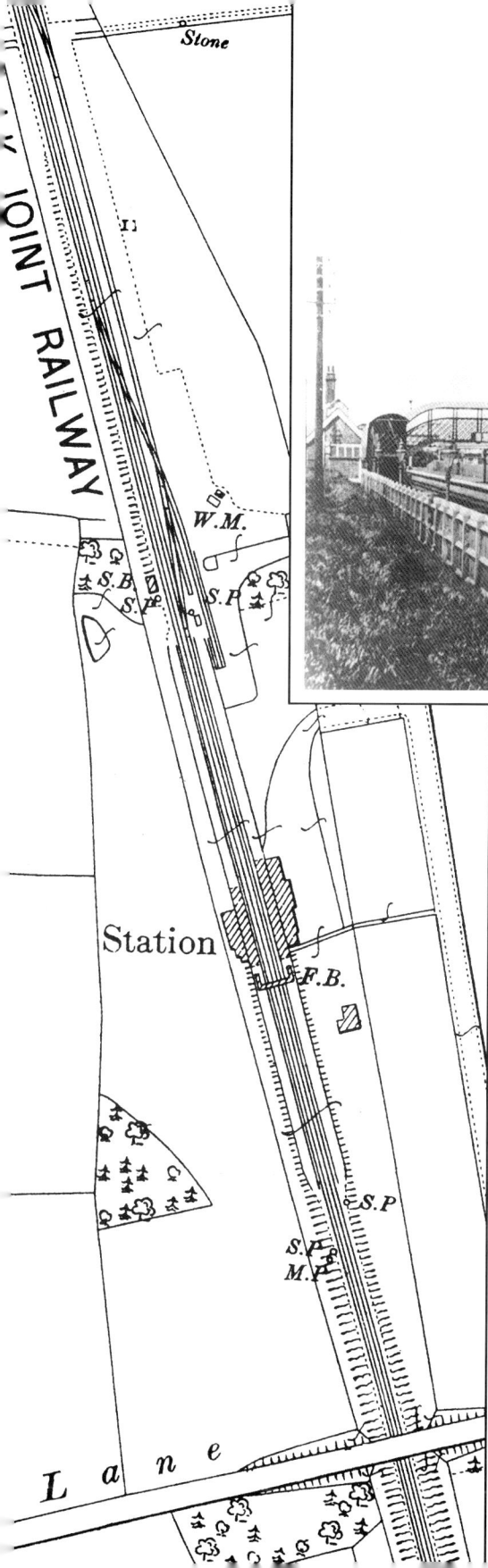

46. We are looking northwards through the station in the early days, with meticulously neat fencing and not a weed to be seen on the platform surface. Over to the right, the fine house provided for the station master overlooks the site.
(Lens of Sutton coll.)

XI. The layout of the station and goods yard, serving a parish of 618 souls, is shown as it appeared shortly after opening in this 1905 edition plan.

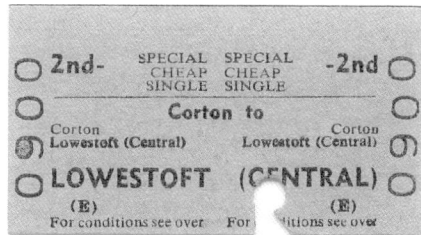

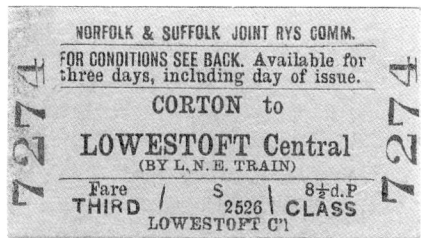

← 47.   The former station master's house sets the scene as class J17 0-6-0 no. 65567 heads south with a trainload of track panels in October 1960. At this time the closed Yarmouth to Beccles line was being lifted, and much of the recovered track was sent to the yard at Lowestoft North for sorting. In the distance, a DMU stands underneath the station footbridge. (G.R.Siviour)

← 48.   Again, we are looking northwards, and everything is still neat and tidy in September 1962, although the footbridge has lost its roof. Let us savour the scene while we can, for the spiral of decay will soon set in. Goods traffic was withdrawn in July 1964, the signal box closed on 20th January 1965, the station became unstaffed from 12th September 1966 and the track was singled in 1967. (E.Tuddenham/ P.J.Bower and M&GN Circle)

49.   All the stations between Gorleston North and Lowestoft North provided separate waiting rooms for different categories of passengers. There was a Ladies Waiting Room, a First Class Ladies Waiting Room, a General Waiting Room and a First Class Waiting Room, each with their function etched into the glass windows. The winter sunshine illuminates the "Booking Hall and General Waiting Room" on 27th February 1967, but by this time the buildings were firmly locked, and the wooden bench under the canopy provides the only comfort for waiting passengers.
(Railway Record of the British Isles/G.L.Pring)

50.   After the line had been reduced to a single track, all trains used the western platform, where there was no shelter at all. Several passengers are boarding a "last day" train for Yarmouth, and all appear to be "genuine" travellers, rather than members of the railway enthusiast fraternity. (R.J.Adderson)

51.   Having avoided the demolition gangs, the station building was restored and converted into a dwelling. As such, it was the only major building on the whole route to survive into the 21st century. Despite a few changes, a comparison with picture 45 will show that the building still bears a striking resemblance to that at neighbouring Hopton. (G.L.Kenworthy)

S.P

S.P

S.P

S.P

XII. This was another location where traffic never reached anticipated levels. Passenger facilities were similar to those at the other stations; accommodation was even provided for a lavatory attendant. This 1905 edition plan indicates the area to the east of the line, used by Oliver, the contractor who constructed the line, as a works depot. The footbridge at the northern end of the site was provided

Lowestoft
North Station

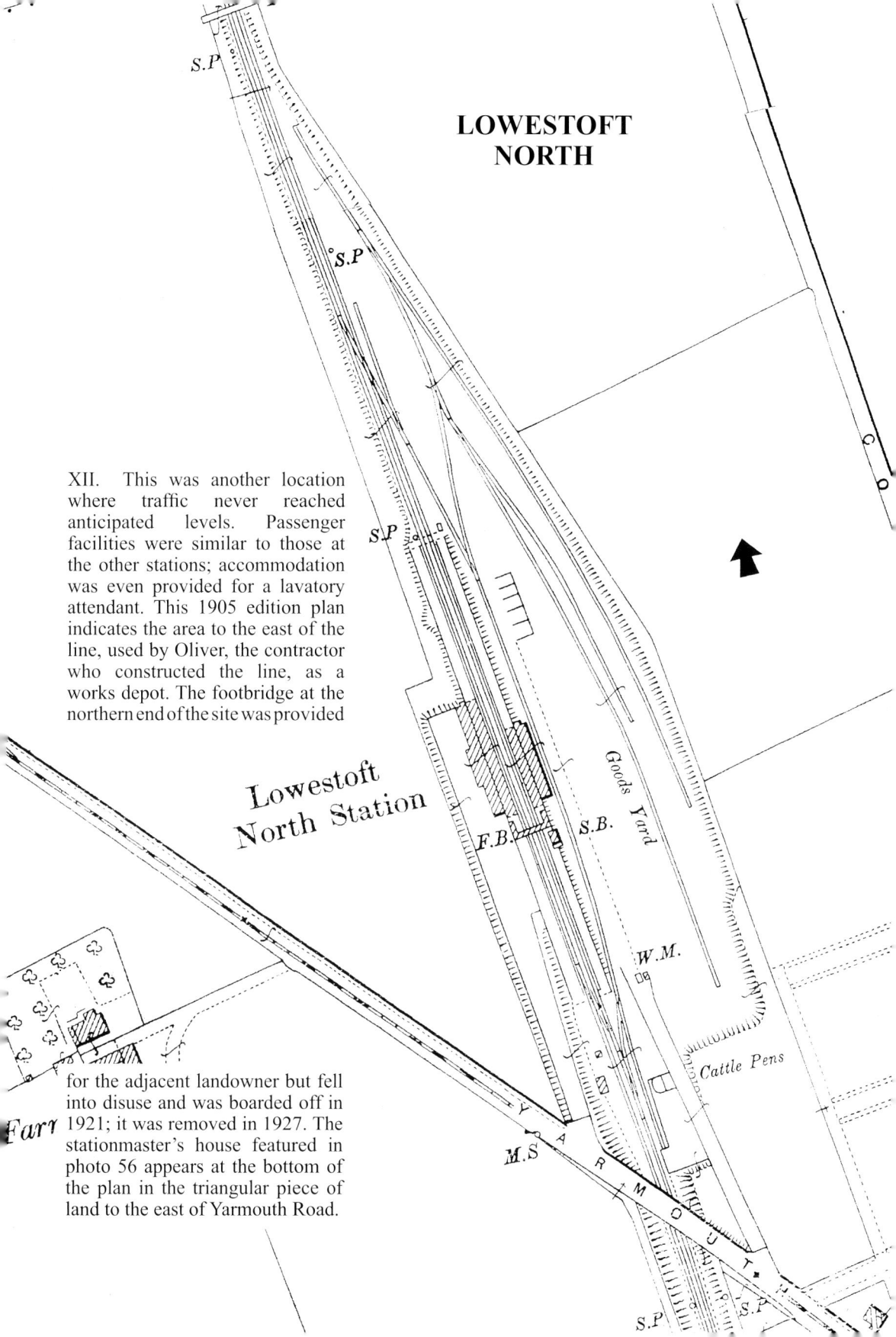

Goods Yard

F.B.   S.B.

W.M.

Cattle Pens

Farr

for the adjacent landowner but fell into disuse and was boarded off in 1921; it was removed in 1927. The stationmaster's house featured in photo 56 appears at the bottom of the plan in the triangular piece of land to the east of Yarmouth Road.

M.S

YARMOUTH

S.P   S.P

52. Here is the station looking northwards shortly after it opened. Again, it is a spacious scene of long platforms with an imposing range of station buildings; a situation that would change only in detail over the next 60 years. The Minutes for January 1902 record the decision to provide electric lighting here from the outset, even though gas installation would have been cheaper – there were to be no economies in the building of this new railway! Transport in this part of the town underwent a revolution in the Summer of 1903, as the coming of the railway coincided with the opening of the Lowestoft Corporation Tramways line which crossed the railway bridge on Yarmouth Road. (M&GN Trust)

53. The holiday industry brought lengthy trains to the line on Summer Saturdays during the 1950s. Class D16/3 4-4-0 no. 62524 passes the station with the 1.43 pm "Holiday Camps Express" from Gorleston to Liverpool Street on 31st August 1957. Each Saturday that summer, the local passenger service was augmented by two such trains to Liverpool Street, with four bringing holidaymakers in the opposite direction. In addition there was a train in each direction serving Derby and Leicester, as well as a through train to York. Camping coach no. 123 helps the railway to cater for the influx of Summer visitors. (B.Harrison)

54. No. 123 was replaced by Pullman camping coach no. 171 in the early 1960s. This twelve-wheeled vehicle dated back to 1917, and in its heyday had formed part of the Continental expresses from Victoria to Dover, including the "Golden Arrow" between 1946 and 1951. By contrast, its predecessor had led a far less glamorous existence, spending the best part of 40 years carrying third class passengers over the GER system. Additional sidings have been installed in the expanse of railway land to the east and are being used as a centre for dealing with track recovered from the Yarmouth to Beccles line. (W.J.Naunton)

55.   The station has quite a prosperous appearance as we look across from the long approach road on 27th February 1967. Admittedly, public access is now through a side gate rather than the booking hall, which has been locked out of use since the staff were withdrawn some six months previously, but there are still wagons in the goods yard, a footbridge linking the platforms, and a signal box. (Railway Record of the British Isles/G.L.Pring)

56.   By the end of the twentieth century the site of the station had disappeared under housing development, and was virtually unrecognisable. However, the station master's house remained, probably because it was isolated from the railway in its position at the corner of Station Road. It had changed little in 2007, and still bore a strong resemblance to its counterpart at Corton, which we saw in pictures 46 and 47. (G.L.Kenworthy)

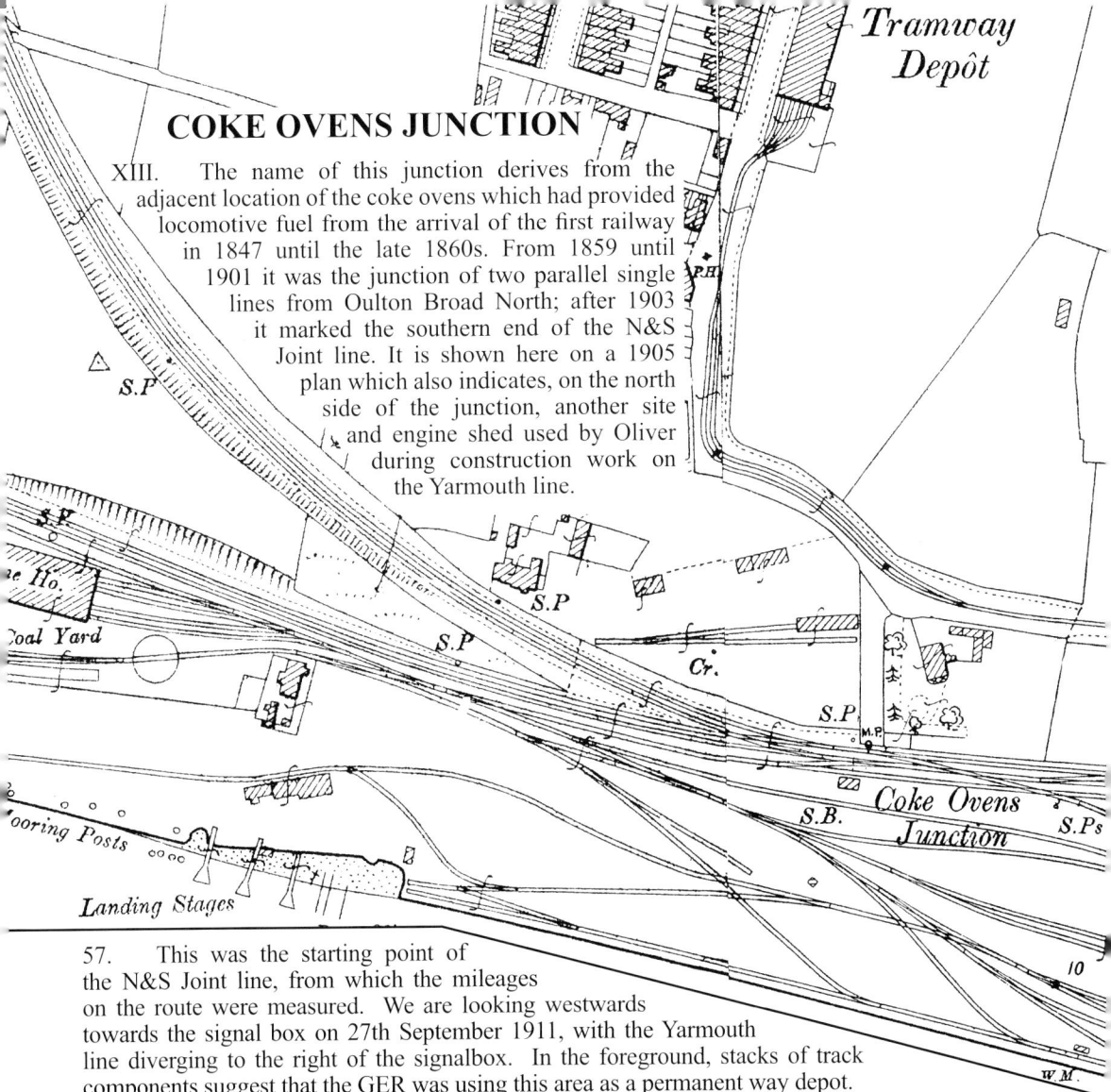

COKE OVENS JUNCTION

XIII. The name of this junction derives from the adjacent location of the coke ovens which had provided locomotive fuel from the arrival of the first railway in 1847 until the late 1860s. From 1859 until 1901 it was the junction of two parallel single lines from Oulton Broad North; after 1903 it marked the southern end of the N&S Joint line. It is shown here on a 1905 plan which also indicates, on the north side of the junction, another site and engine shed used by Oliver during construction work on the Yarmouth line.

57. This was the starting point of the N&S Joint line, from which the mileages on the route were measured. We are looking westwards towards the signal box on 27th September 1911, with the Yarmouth line diverging to the right of the signalbox. In the foreground, stacks of track components suggest that the GER was using this area as a permanent way depot. (GERS/Windwood Collection)

← 58. In later years further sidings were installed in the area formerly occupied by the contractor, and during 1958 they were briefly occupied by railbus no SC79959. This was one of two such vehicles whose chassis, having been built in Bristol, were brought to Lowestoft by road to be united with their bodies. These had been constructed at the Eastern Coach Works factory, which can be seen to the left of our picture. One, if not both, of the completed vehicles reached the railway system by means of a temporary connection slewed into the Yarmouth line. They were destined to operate on British Railways for less than a decade, owing to the closures of the rural branch lines for which they were intended. The classic combination of Bristol chassis and ECW body was, of course, far more successful in the bus industry. (NRS Archive)

← 59. As we can see here, the sidings were regularly used during the 1950s for stabling coaches. On this occasion, class J17 0-6-0 no. 65588 has eased up to an engineers' Grampus wagon, which appears to have pushed back the buffer stops by a few feet as the result of over-vigorous shunting. In the background a line of brand new Lodekka buses have emerged from the Eastern Coach Works factory and await delivery to their new owners.
(B.Laughland)

60.   During the last few weeks of services, a Cravens DMU from Yarmouth approaches the level crossing at Laundry Lane, just a quarter of a mile from the junction. In the eleven miles between here and Nelson Road Junction there were 48 bridges, and just this one public level crossing, a fact that again illustrates the extent of the civil engineering work needed to construct the line. The little hut was saved from demolition and spent many years at the East Anglian Transport Museum at nearby Carlton Colville, before being moved to the Mid Norfolk Railway in 2003. (M.J.Wilson)

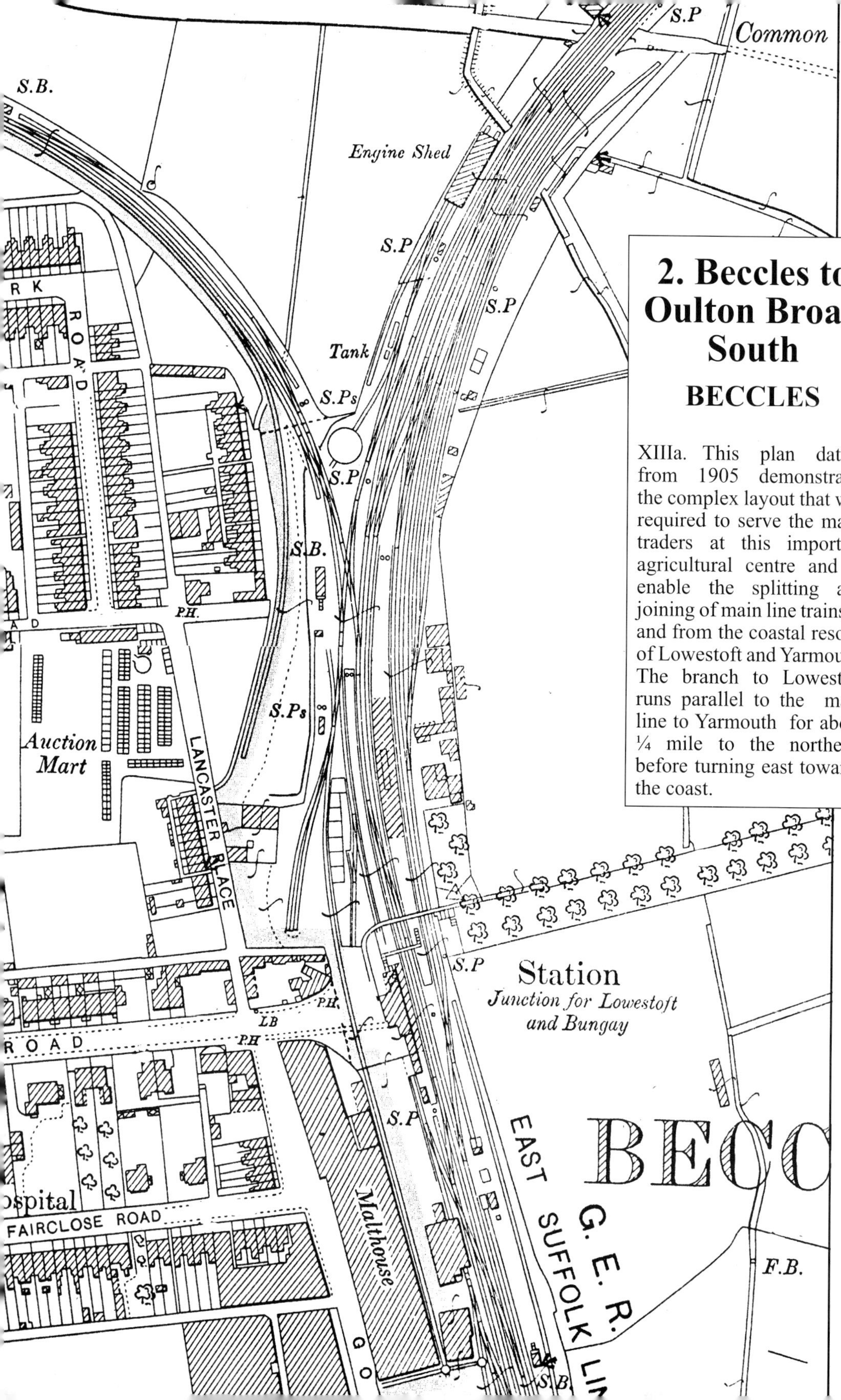

S.P — Common

S.B.

Engine Shed

S.P

S.P

Tank

S.Ps

S.P

S.B.

P.H.

S.Ps

Auction Mart

R K ROAD

LANCASTER PLACE

S.P

Station
Junction for Lowestoft and Bungay

ROAD

P.H.

LB

P.H.

S.P

ospital

FAIRCLOSE ROAD

Malthouse

BEC...

EAST SUFFOLK LIN...

G. E. R.

S.B.

F.B.

2. Beccles to Oulton Broad South

BECCLES

XIIIa. This plan dating from 1905 demonstrates the complex layout that was required to serve the many traders at this important agricultural centre and to enable the splitting and joining of main line trains to and from the coastal resorts of Lowestoft and Yarmouth. The branch to Lowestoft runs parallel to the main line to Yarmouth for about ¼ mile to the northeast before turning east towards the coast.

61.   We have to be grateful to the photographer who carried his heavy equipment to the top of a water tank in order to obtain this panorama of the north end of the station on 10th October 1911. The Waveney Valley branch heads away to the west, while the lines to Yarmouth and Lowestoft curve round to the east, parting company with each other just out of the picture. In the middle distance, a tank locomotive stands at the coaling stage outside the engine shed. In 2008 there was just a single track running through this area – a striking contrast with the amount of land that the railway occupied in its heyday. (GERS/Windwood Collection)

62.   Class F5 2-4-2T no. 67199 stands in the platform on 27th July 1954 with an afternoon push-pull working to Lowestoft. Such trains were a common sight in the area at this time, sometimes on diagrams including local trains on all three sides of the Yarmouth-Beccles-Lowestoft triangle. (G.R.Siviour)

← 63. One day in the late 1950s, Britannia class 4-6-2 no. 70012 *John of Gaunt* is backing into platform 4 to collect the Lowestoft portion of a train to London, which it will then add to the Yarmouth coaches for the onward journey. Meanwhile, three members of the station staff are taking full advantage of the unusual barrow bridge to transfer some cumbersome items between the platforms. (R.J.Adderson coll.)

← 64. The signal shows that class J15 0-6-0 no. 65460 will be taking the Lowestoft line with its goods train, which includes traffic from the Waveney Valley line. It is October 1960 and the station retains the "feel" of a busy country junction, even though the direct line to Yarmouth had closed a year earlier and is now host only to demolition trains, while the Waveney Valley branch had lost its passenger service in January 1953. (G.R.Siviour)

65. There have been regular calls for the reinstatement of a loop here, which would allow a more frequent service on the East Suffolk line by breaking up the long single-track section between Oulton Broad and Halesworth. A class 170 arrives at the neglected looking station with a train from Lowestoft to Liverpool Street in March 2008. (G.L.Kenworthy)

Other pictures are featured in our earlier volumes *Saxmundham to Yarmouth* and *Tivetshall to Beccles*.

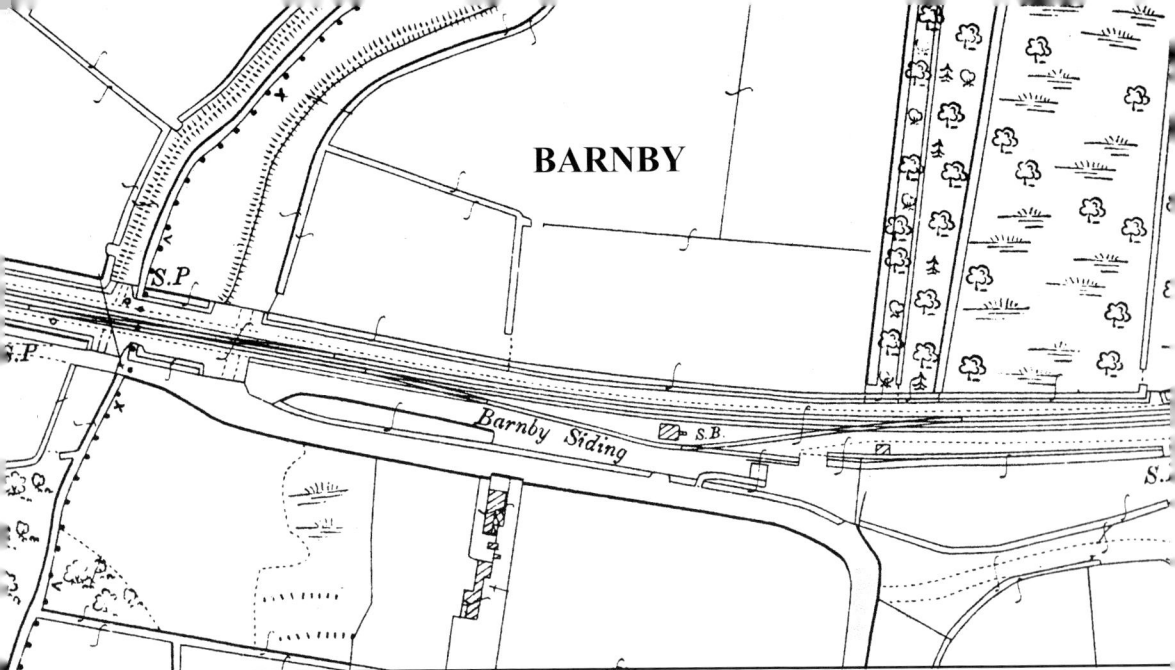

BARNBY

Barnby Siding
S.B.

XIV.   The location is shown as it appeared in 1905. The branch was originally single line at this point but in the early 1880s it was deemed necessary to provide a crossing loop. The goods yard sidings and extension of the loop followed in 1887.

66.   This is Barnby around 1960: just a signal box, a long siding with hard standing for road transport, and the loading dock on which the photographer is standing, looking towards Beccles. Wayside sidings such as this were rare in this part of East Anglia, although fairly common in the fenland to the west. Other places have their "Station Road" as a reminder of long-vanished facilities: here in 2008 "Siding Road" still recalled Barnby's status in the railway hierarchy. (B.Laughland)

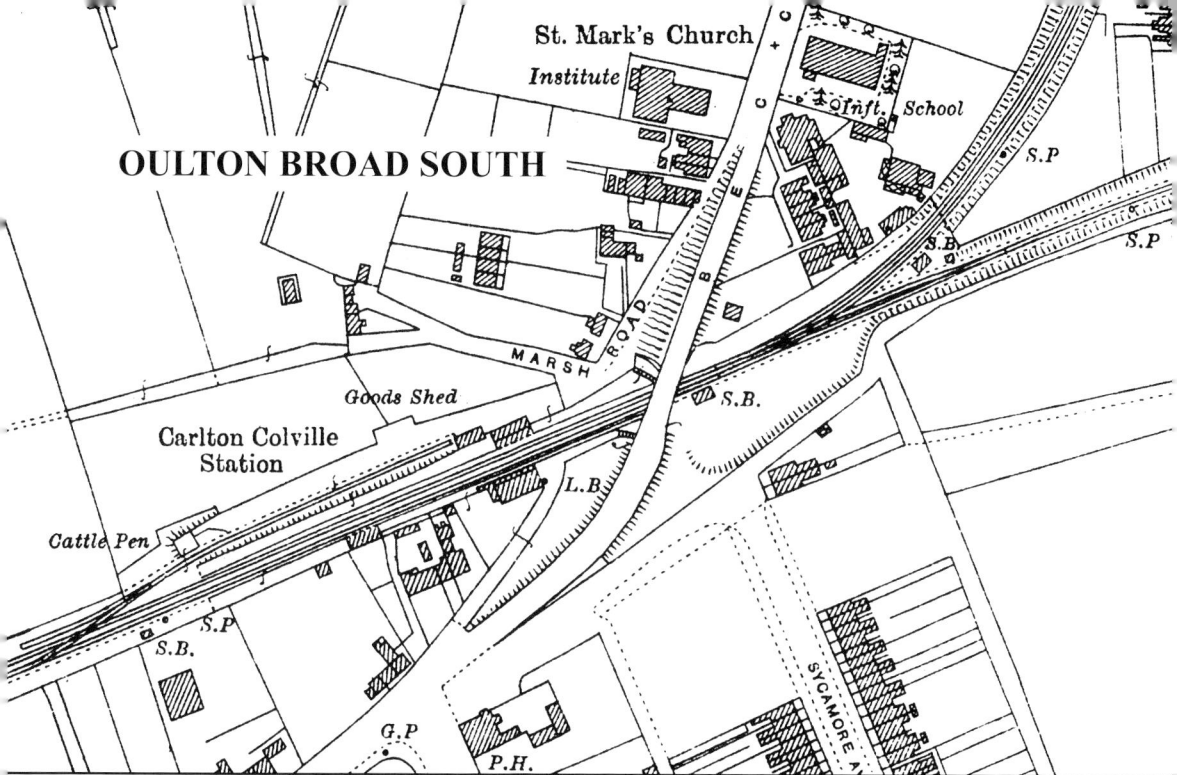

OULTON BROAD SOUTH

St. Mark's Church
Institute
Inft. School

Goods Shed

Carlton Colville
Station

Cattle Pen

S.P
S.B.

G.P
P.H.

XV.   This station was known as Carlton Colville from its opening in 1859 until September 1927, a year or so after the revision date of this 1927 edition plan. The sharp diversion northwards from the originally intended passenger route at the eastern end of the station should be noted, the original formation continuing due east and subsequently providing access for goods traffic to the south side of Lake Lothing.

67.   Here is an overall view of the station from the west, on 4th October 1911, with the entrance to the small goods yard on the left. The "kink" in the track at the platform end results from the realignment necessary when the line was doubled some four years earlier. The LNER changed the name to the more commercially attractive Oulton Broad South. (GERS/Windwood Collection)

68. A Cravens DMU does a little business at the station before setting off for Beccles on a Summer day in the late 1950s. It is standing at the platform provided when the line was opened, and the design of the station building is similar to several others on the East Suffolk line. To the left of the picture we have a glimpse of the camping coach which was based here at the time. (NRS Archive)

69. No 170206 has arrived on a service from London on 13th February 2008. Sadly, the number of passengers alighting is not typical – they are transferring to buses for the last stage of their journey to Lowestoft, as the line beyond is closed owing to engineering work on the swing bridge. (R.J.Adderson)

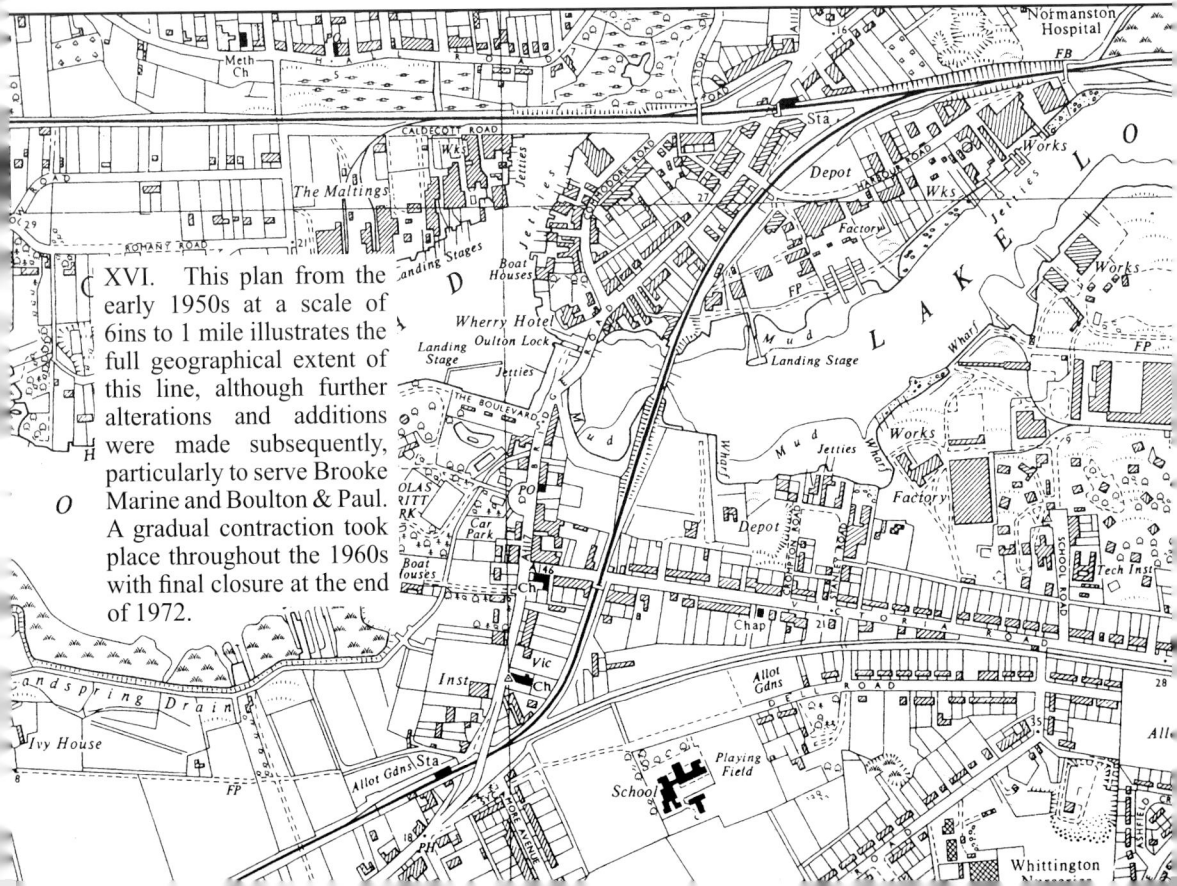

XVI. This plan from the early 1950s at a scale of 6ins to 1 mile illustrates the full geographical extent of this line, although further alterations and additions were made subsequently, particularly to serve Brooke Marine and Boulton & Paul. A gradual contraction took place throughout the 1960s with final closure at the end of 1972.

3. Oulton Broad South to Lowestoft South Side
LOWESTOFT SOUTH SIDE

70.   Looking eastwards from the road bridge on 4th October 1911, we have a good view of the junction. Reflecting the priorities of the original 1856 Act, the South Side branch continues straight ahead, whilst the main line curves sharply to the left past the signal box. The roof of the earlier Junction signal box, replaced in 1907 when the line was doubled, is in the foreground. (GERS/Windwood Collection)

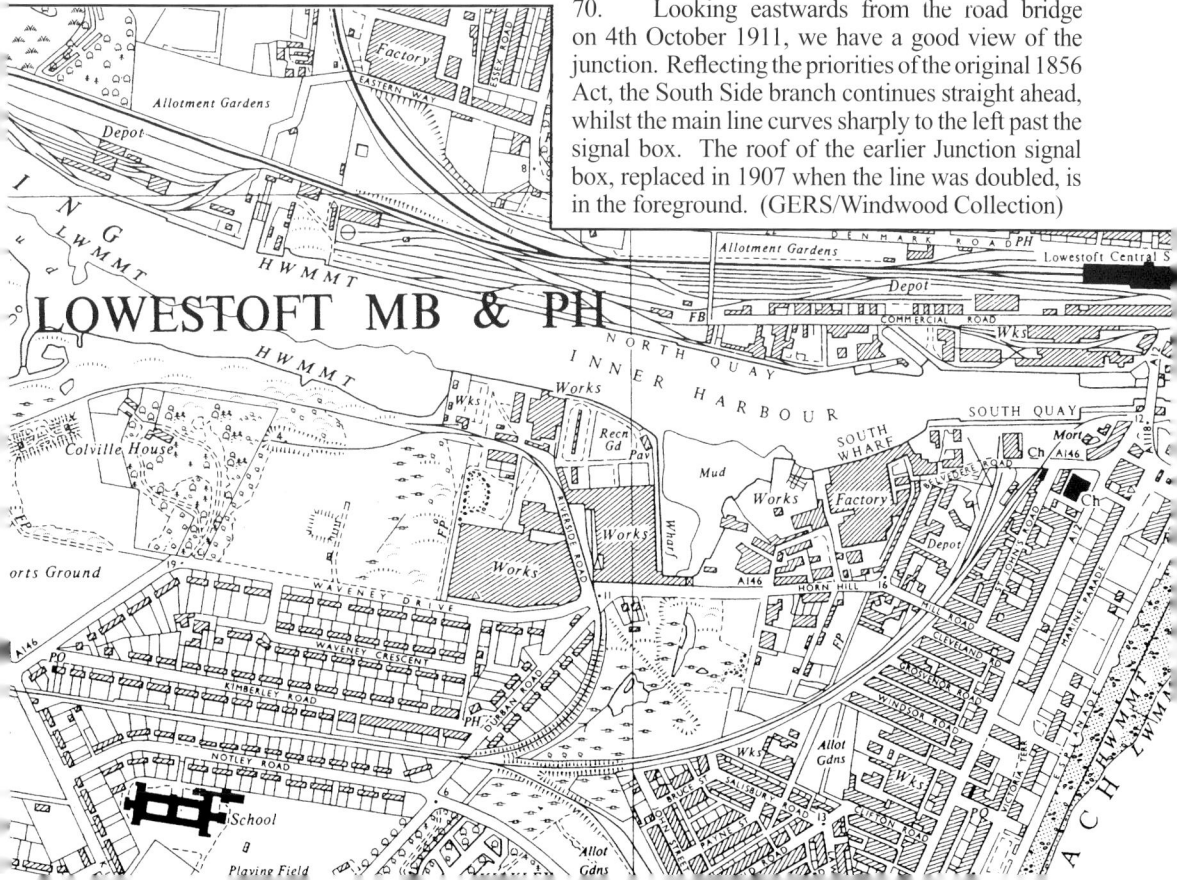

71. A class 03 shunter makes its way back towards the junction during the late 1960s. The houses to the left are on Kimberley Road; those to the right are a later development on Notley Road. In earlier days, the residents of the former obviously had reservations about the nearby railway – a 1918 Licence Agreement between the GER and the local councils prohibited locomotives from standing or "taking in water" within fifty yards of Kimberley Road. This is a somewhat vague clause, as the road and railway ran parallel to each other, and almost exactly fifty yards apart. (I.C.Allen/Transport Treasury)

72. From 1916 onwards, the branch forked into three just over a mile from the main line, adjacent to the level crossing over Durban Road. This was the three-way junction as it appeared around 1960. The line in the centre is the original route to Lowestoft South Side, around half a mile away, while that to the right provides access to Kirkley Goods Depot – four sidings which had been provided in 1907 and were closed at the beginning of 1966. The third line had been added in 1916 to serve the factory of Maconochie Brothers Ltd, the family company which was largely responsible for the development of this part of the town. As we shall see, this line was later extended to serve various industrial premises on the south bank of Lake Lothing. (NRS Archive)

73.   The level crossing with Durban Road intersected the junction, and right up to the closure a flagman usually controlled the crossing when a train was passing. Duly protected, a class 03 curves round from the northernmost line around 1967. The short spur to Kirkley has been lifted, but there are still wagons on the line to South Side. (I.C.Allen/Transport Treasury)

74.   Looking northwards from Mill Road bridge, we have our first glimpse of the terminus at Lowestoft South Side, even though the track layout is not readily apparent from this photograph, which was taken in the aftermath of the disastrous North Sea floods of 1953. Despite sweeping changes elsewhere in South Lowestoft, this area was still recognisable in 2008, serving as a car park, whilst the houses to the right had scarcely changed. (G.L.Kenworthy coll.)

75.   Class J17 0-6-0 no.65558 stands at the neglected-looking Lowestoft South Side after a trip down the branch during the 1950s. Behind it, two wagons stand on one of the lines that provided access to the quayside sidings, originally by means of wagon turntables but later using conventional pointwork. (I.C.Allen/Transport Treasury)

76.   Once steam had gone, small diesel shunters of class 03 and 05 operated the South Side network in the declining years. During the early 1960s, one of the 05s working from Lowestoft shed has reached South Side yard, which is still active with coal traffic. It is standing on the more westerly of the lines that continued through the yard to serve the quayside and various industrial concerns. The section of line between here and Durban Road closed on 6th November 1967, and the track was lifted a year or so later. (NRS Archive)

77.	Now we retrace our steps to Durban Road for a trip down the northern branch. One day during the 1950s, a flagman is in action again, as class J17 0-6-0 no. 65559 holds up road traffic on Waveney Drive, the main road between Oulton Broad and South Lowestoft. A road sweeper rests from his labours to watch the train go by. The building to the right of the engine is the Co-op factory, which in its original ownership as Maconochies works had been the destination of the branch when it opened in 1916. (I.C.Allen/Transport Treasury)

78.	As more industries grew up in the area, the line was extended to serve them. It was diverted to serve the new Brooke Marine shipyard during the 1950s, and a siding was provided for the timber works of Boulton & Paul (Lowestoft) Ltd as late as 1961. Class J17 no. 65558 was photographed on Riverside Road, returning from the dockland lines with a short goods train, again during the 1950s. Some years later the demolition of the tower to the right of the road caused a minor crisis, when the debris fell across the railway line, marooning a train in the B&P yard at the far end of the line. (W.J.Naunton)

79. Traffic from Boulton & Paul kept the line open into the 1970s, by which time it had become something of an anachronism. Surrounded by contemporary cars, D2037 propels a train along Riverside Road towards the Boulton & Paul yard on 23rd June 1970. At this time the main traffic flow consisted of window components being sent to the firm's Melton Mowbray works for assembly into finished window units. (R.J.Adderson)

80. During the final years, an 03 has arrived at the Boulton & Paul yard, where it meets the company's Baguley 0-4-0 diesel shunter. After the line closed on 31st December 1972, this engine was transferred to the owner's Norwich premises, where it survived until 1986. Major redevelopment of the area in the early 21st century obliterated most remaining traces of the South Side lines, together with the industrial premises they served. (I.C.Allen/Transport Treasury)

4. Oulton Broad South to Lowestoft Central

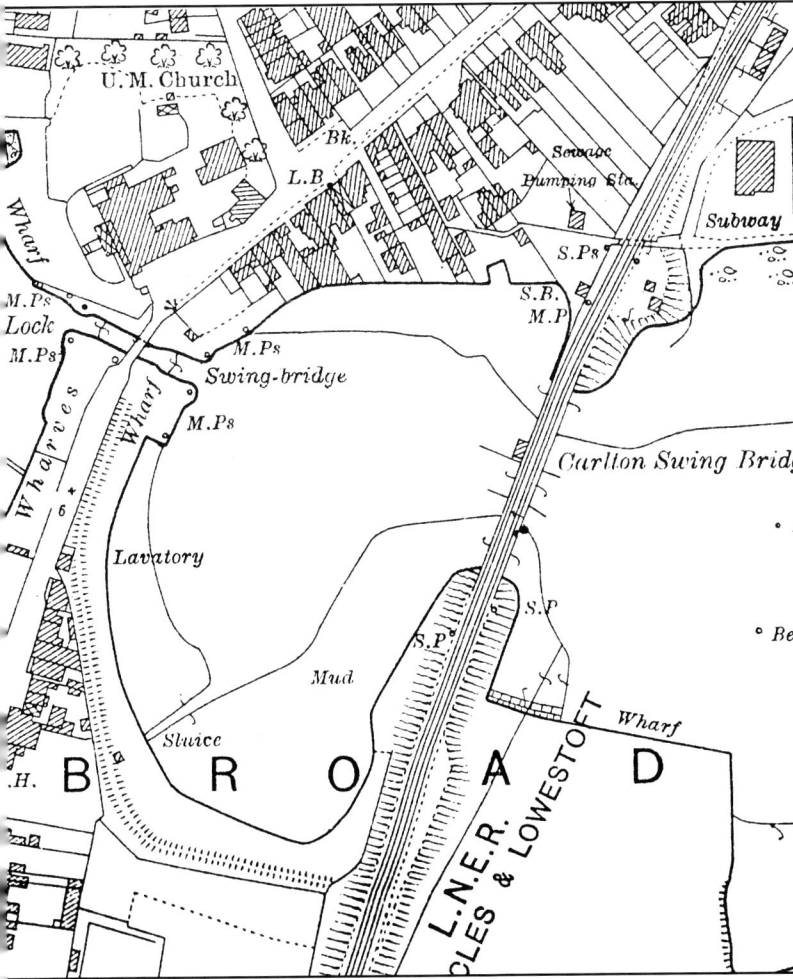

OULTON BROAD SWING BRIDGE

XVII. The position of the double track swing bridge which replaced the original single line version in 1907 is shown on this 1927 edition. Its location prior to rebuilding was a few yards to the east.

81. The railway crossed the western end of Lake Lothing on a wooden trestle bridge, equipped with a swinging span to allow free passage to shipping. This structure, seen here from the southwest, remained in use until it was replaced by a modern double-track swing bridge in 1907. The first train over the new bridge was the 7.23 am from Lowestoft on 10th November of that year. (A.R.Taylor coll.)

← 82. Class B17 4-6-0 no. 61660 *Hull City* heads an up express between the swing bridge and Victoria Road level crossing on a snowy day in 1959. The replacement bridge had been built just to the west of its predecessor, necessitating a reverse curve in the track to reach the new alignment. (R.W.Moore)

← 83. No 37050 crosses the swing bridge with the 17.00 train from Liverpool Street on 1st April 1984. A few weeks later this service, together with the morning up train, ran for the last time. As a result the East Suffolk line was served only by local trains, a situation which was to last for the next 15 years. In the foreground, the abandoned *Yellowtail* sums up the decline of Lowestoft's once thriving fishing industry. (R.J.Adderson)

84.   Under a threatening sky, a class 101 DMU rattles over the bridge with a train for Ipswich on 23rd June 1984. A red flag fluttering above the bridge warns river users of the possible obstruction to their passage. The number of onlookers, especially on the signal box, confirms that this photograph was taken during a Norfolk Railway Society visit to the location. (D.C.Pearce)

OULTON BROAD NORTH JUNCTION

Oulton Broad Station

Timber Yard

LOTHING STREET

HARBOUR ROAD

Iron Foundry

Shipbuilding Yard

High Water Mark

M.P.

Jetty

Oulton Works (Implements)

Bo

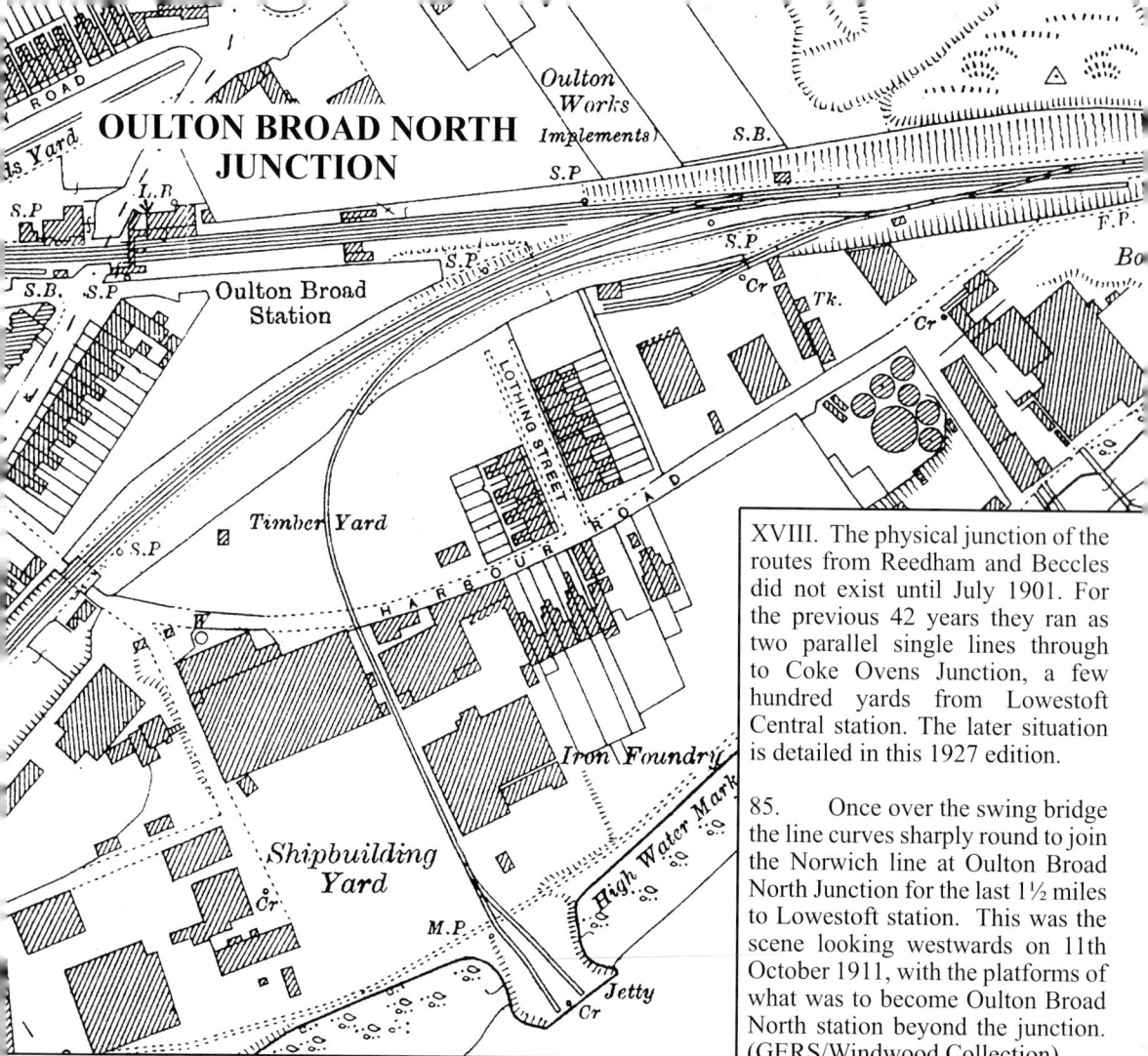

XVIII. The physical junction of the routes from Reedham and Beccles did not exist until July 1901. For the previous 42 years they ran as two parallel single lines through to Coke Ovens Junction, a few hundred yards from Lowestoft Central station. The later situation is detailed in this 1927 edition.

85. Once over the swing bridge the line curves sharply round to join the Norwich line at Oulton Broad North Junction for the last 1½ miles to Lowestoft station. This was the scene looking westwards on 11th October 1911, with the platforms of what was to become Oulton Broad North station beyond the junction. (GERS/Windwood Collection)

86.   A minor road crossed the line at Gravel Pit level crossing, situated on the curve between the swing bridge and the junction. Here we are looking southwards towards the swing bridge in around 1960, with the distant bridge house visible above the crossing gates. The two-storey crossing-keeper's house, small hut, ground frame and the level crossing gates themselves are a reminder of the facilities that the railway provided even at fairly unimportant crossings such as this. (S.Jones)

87.   Heading for Ipswich, no. 150227 takes the East Suffolk line on 19th June 2001. The rural appearance of the scene is deceptive, for we are in a crowded residential area, and the trees hide the commercial and industrial activity on the dockside. (S.McNae)

M.Ps

on

Beacon

I. *·· ·N·* *G·*

Beacon

Gantry

New Creosoting Depôt

W.M.

M.P

N O R

M.P

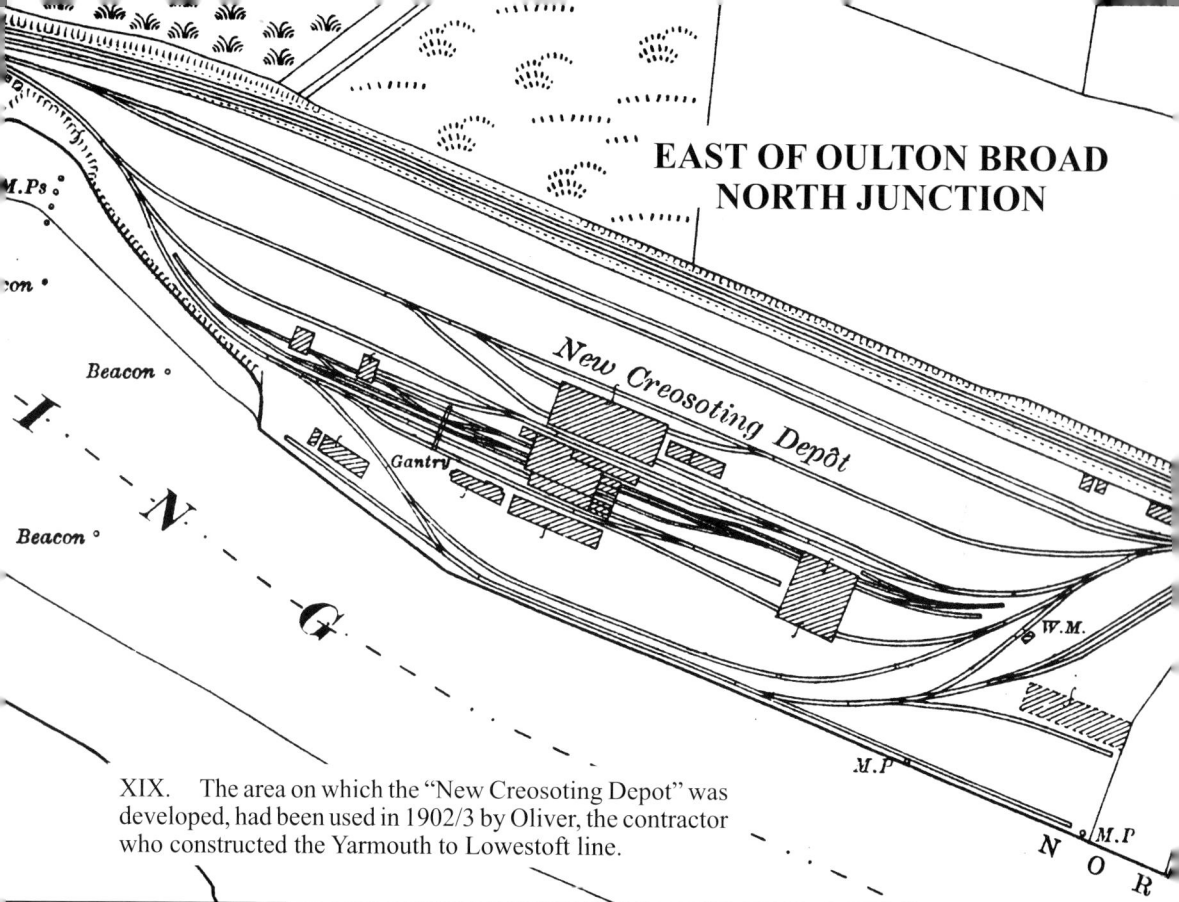

XIX.   The area on which the "New Creosoting Depot" was developed, had been used in 1902/3 by Oliver, the contractor who constructed the Yarmouth to Lowestoft line.

88.   As we have seen in picture 57, there were indications that the site used for permanent way materials adjacent to Coke Ovens Junction was becoming hopelessly congested. In 1913/4 the GER established a dedicated sleeper depot further to the west, on 15-acre site adjoining Lake Lothing. The passing traveller could scarcely miss this installation, with the towering stacks of sleepers, the pungent aroma of creosote, and maybe a Sentinel loco shuffling around the site. We can't provide the smell, but here is Sentinel no. 40 in typical surroundings within the complex during the 1950s. In 1957 it was reported that some 405,000 sleepers were treated here annually, a process using no less than 800,000 gallons of creosote. (I.C.Allen/Transport Treasury)

89.   Britannia class 4-6-2 no. 70002 *Geoffrey Chaucer* passes the sleeper depot headshunt as it approaches Oulton Broad North Junction with an up express around 1959. (B.Laughland)

90.   Timber for the works was imported from various European countries, notably the Baltic region, and was brought by sea to a 1000ft. long quay on the south side of the depot. By 1957 additional supplies from the USA and Canada were landed at either London or Immingham docks and transported by rail to Lowestoft. No.40 is shunting on the quayside on 28th May 1960, although on this occasion the maritime interest is provided by what appears to be an ancient dredger, rather than a timber ship. (H.N.James/ITM coll.)

91.   Just under half a mile of 3ft. gauge track supplemented the standard gauge lines within the works, and was used for carting materials around the site. *Monty*, a 4-wheeled Ruston & Hornsby diesel locomotive dating from 1944, stands outside the creosoting shed on 28th May 1960, with standard gauge tracks in the foreground. (A.W.E.Hoskins)

92.   *Billy*, a 4-wheeled petrol engine built by Motor Rail Ltd in 1920, had been delivered new to the sleeper depot in 1920 for use on the 3' gauge system. It, too, was photographed with the darkness of the creosoting shed as a background. On this day, 17th March 1962, the engine, although very much a spare, is having a rare outing whilst *Monty* undergoes repairs in the Harbour works. (C.Fisher)

93.   Here is *Monty* again, this time on 30th May 1964. It is inside the engine shed, which it shared with the Sentinel shunters used in the depot. After the sleeper depot closed, this engine was sold for further use, but the older *Billy* was less fortunate, being scrapped on site. (R.Harrison)

94.   The Sentinel locomotives continued to shunt at the sleeper depot until it closed in 1964, and thus became the last British Railways steam engines to operate in East Anglia on a regular basis. Nos 7 and 40 stand outside the engine shed on 30th May 1964. (R. Harrison)

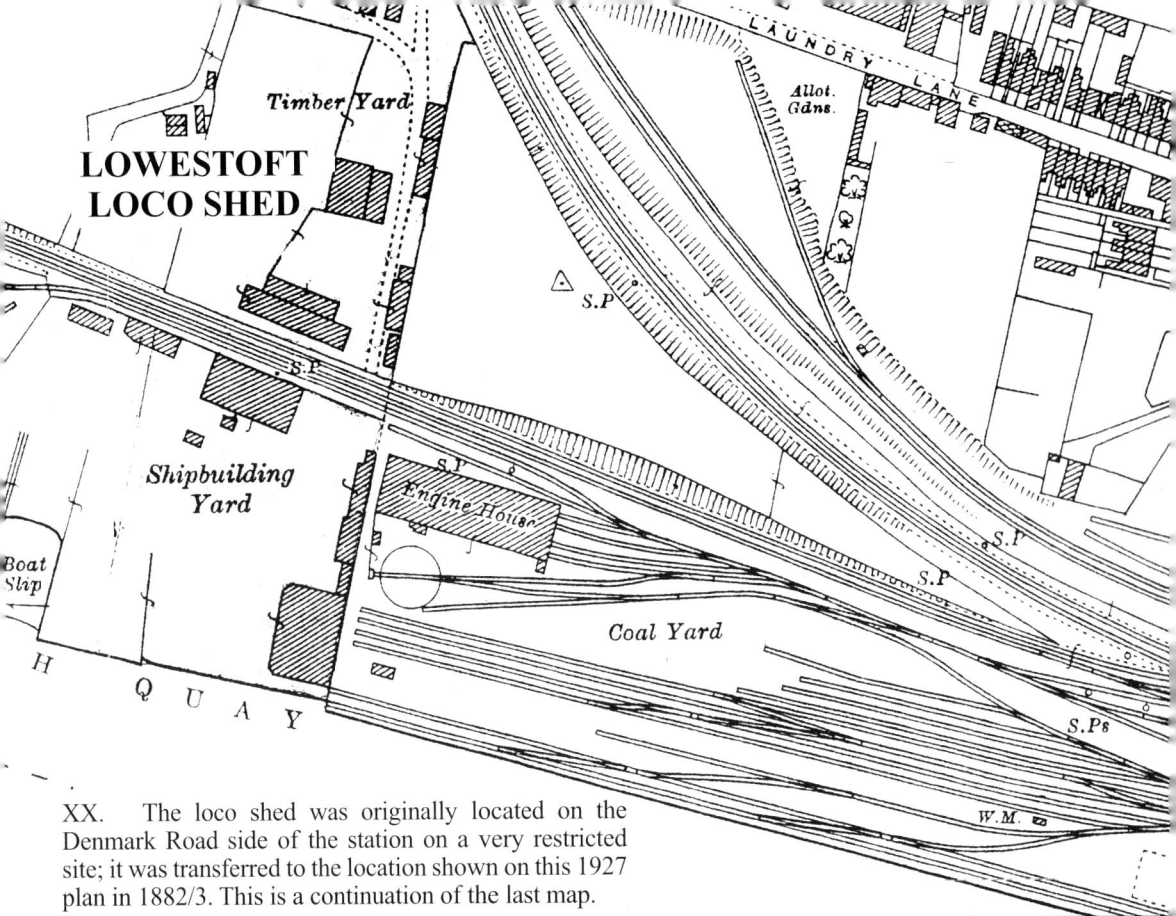

LOWESTOFT
LOCO SHED

Timber Yard

Shipbuilding
Yard

Boat
Slip

Engine House

Coal Yard

H Q U A Y

LAUNDRY LANE

Allot.
Gdns.

S.P.

S.P.

S.P.

S.P.

S.P.

S.Ps

W.M.

XX.   The loco shed was originally located on the Denmark Road side of the station on a very restricted site; it was transferred to the location shown on this 1927 plan in 1882/3. This is a continuation of the last map.

95.   We are looking eastwards along the main line on 27th September 1911, with four locomotives standing outside the engine shed. For many years water for the engines was obtained from a reservoir to the north of the line, which was fed by a series of pipes leading from nearby springs. (GERS/Windwood Collection)

96.   The shed was coded 32C in British Railways days, but the arrival of the diesels took away much of the work done by the engines allocated there. By May 1960 the steam era was almost over, and a solitary class J20 0-6-0 is outnumbered by Brush Type 2 diesels. The shed closed to steam later that year, but continued to house a few diesel shunters until 1962. (W.J.Naunton)

97.   During the winter of 1963/4 the shed again provided the backdrop for steam locomotives, when three class B1 4-6-0s returned to the area to provide carriage heating, alternating between Norwich, Lowestoft and Yarmouth. One of the trio, Departmental locomotive no. 19 (formerly no. 61204) stands on the last remaining siding in the shed yard, while a sturdy gate bars access to the building. (W.J.Naunton)

98.   The shed remained standing into the 1980s, serving for some years as a cattle quarantine station. Redevelopment of the former railway land opened up this view during the Summer of 1978, giving us a good idea of the scale of the building, and particularly the massive water tank at the west end. (R.J.Adderson coll.)

XXI.   By the time of this 1950s plan the station facilities had been expanded on a number of occasions to cater for increases in traffic; the only significant change subsequently was the extension of platforms 3&4. The area of the Harbour Works, on the south side of Commercial Road will be covered photographically as a separate section.

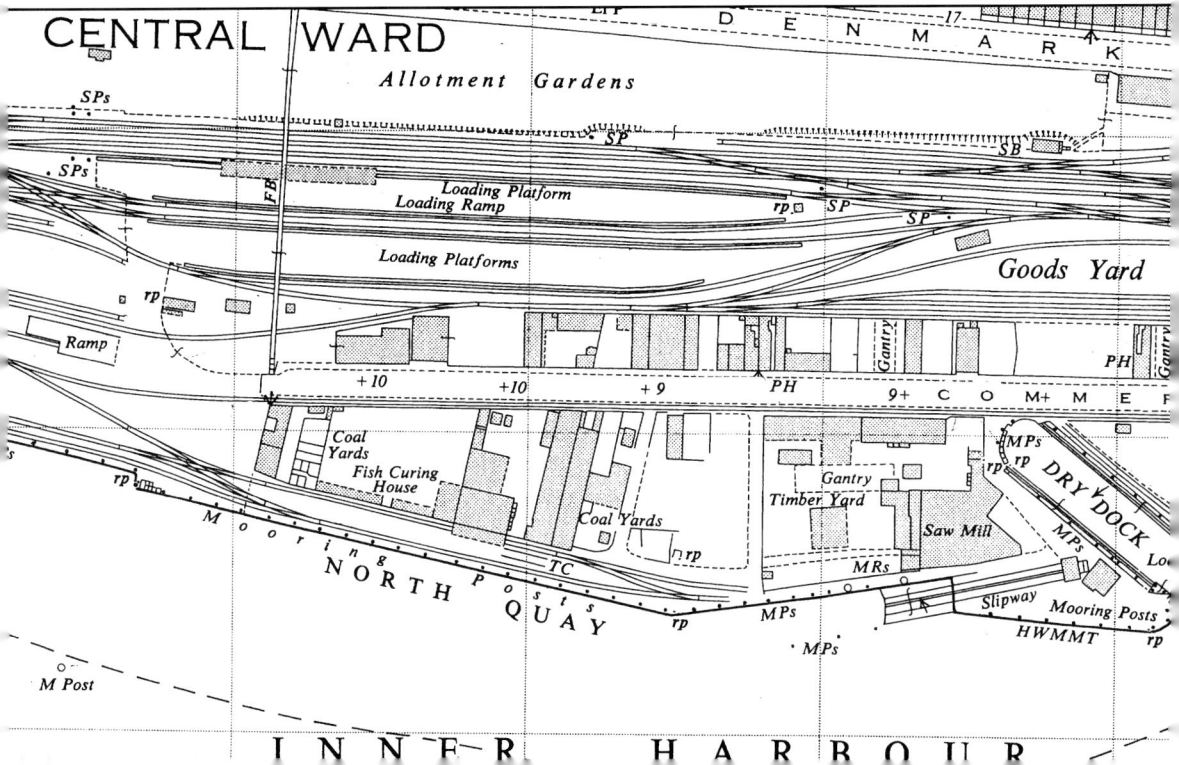

CENTRAL WARD

D E N M A R K

Allotment Gardens

SPs

SP

SB

. SPs

SPs

FB

Loading Platform
Loading Ramp

rp   SP

SP

Loading Platforms

Goods Yard

rp

Ramp

PH

+10   +10   + 9   PH   9+ C O M+ M E F

Coal
Yards

Fish Curing
House

Coal Yards

Gantry

Timber Yard

Saw Mill

MPs

rp

DRY DOCK

MPs

Lo

rp

M o o r i n g

NORTH

P o s t s
QUAY

TC

rp

rp

MPs

MRs

Slipway   Mooring Posts

HWMMT

rp

· MPs

M Post

INNER   HARBOUR

LOWESTOFT CENTRAL

99.   We are looking eastwards towards the station from an elevated viewpoint on 26th September 1911, with the large goods shed to the left of the picture. A rather shabby rake of GER coaches on the left contrasts with the three Midland Railway clerestory-roofed bogie coaches over to the right. These will eventually make their way back to their home system on a through train via Gorleston, Breydon Bridge and the M&GN. Even by this time, the station facilities and track layout had already undergone several improvements and modifications, and this process would continue in the years to come. (GERS/Windwood Collection)

100.　　Now we have an even more elevated view, thanks to a commercial postcard, which a visitor sent home to his family in 1920. "There are a tremendous number of fishing boats here", he wrote. The railway and harbour were in common ownership from the earliest days – the Lowestoft Railway and Harbour Company had been formed in 1845 and the name tells its own story. These twin interests occupy most of the picture, with the quayside lines and covered fish market next to the crowded Trawl basin at the top left, and the station, goods shed and harbour works complex prominent. To the right, the railway owned swing bridge spans the waterway between Lake Lothing and the sea. (R.J.Adderson coll.)

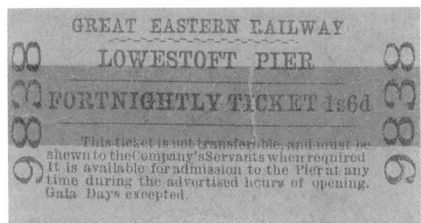

Two items illustrating the varied railway interests at Lowestoft.

Est. 1. 60,000. 10-23.   (18)

MIDLAND & GREAT NORTHERN RAILWAYS
JOINT COMMITTEE.

TO

LOWESTOFT

CENTRAL.

Via Yarmouth Beach & N. & S. Joint

G. E. R.

—

Lowestoft

101.   During the late 1930s, class F4 2-4-2T no. 7175 leaves with a train for the Yarmouth line, passing an incoming express. The last two vehicles are more modern than those behind the engine, and are probably through coaches for the Midlands. This photograph was taken from the footbridge spanning the tracks between Denmark Road and Commercial Road, which provided a handy vantage point for railway observers until it was declared unsafe in the early 2000s. (Lens of Sutton coll.)

← 102. Class F5 2-4-2T no. 67199 takes water at the end of the platform prior to leaving with a train for Yarmouth South Town in July 1954. Small tank locomotives of GER design were commonplace on all the lines radiating from the town until the late 1950s. This platform was later extended to cope with the longer trains which appeared when the Yarmouth/East Suffolk services were diverted this way in 1959. (G.R.Siviour)

← 103. Four long narrow wooden platforms were a feature of the goods yard for many years, helping the railway to cater for the heavy outward fish traffic, and they were at one time provided with lighting so that this important work could carry on round the clock. A class J39 0-6-0 stands at one of these platforms around 1959/60, as the last few boxes of fish are transferred to the train from a lorry. (B.Laughland)

104. Class B17 4-6-0 no. 61664 *Liverpool* gleams in the Winter sunshine as it heads a short goods train out of the station during the 1950s. It is passing underneath the long footbridge, known locally as the "iron bridge", which provided the viewpoint for previous pictures. (W.J.Naunton)

105. The station is situated in the town centre, convenient for the shops and only a short walk from the sea. This was the south-eastern view of the building on 9th September 1969, with the line to the fish markets crossing the main road on the left of the picture. A contemporary police car is worthy of note, as is the Eastern Counties LKH operating Service 3, a circular route via Oulton Broad. (British Railways)

➜ 106. The 14.21 train to Yarmouth stands under the roof on 2nd May 1970. There are only six more round trips to go before another railway passes into history. Just over 11 years earlier, the closure of the M&GN had heralded an era of railway retrenchment, during which some 15 lines had lost their passenger trains in Norfolk and Suffolk alone. The service along the coast to Yarmouth proved to be the last of this series of closures, and the map of passenger lines in the two counties would remain unchanged for many years. (R.J.Adderson)

➜ 107. It is around 8 pm on 12th November 1983, and the station retains much of the old atmosphere. A Class 31 has arrived in platform 4 with the through train from London, whilst a class 101 DMU stands at platform 3, ready to work the last train of the day to Ipswich. (D.C.Pearce)

Departures
Next train from
platform 3 to
Norwich

Lowestoft

150213

ipswich

Departures
Next train from
platform 2 to
Ipswich

153314

← 108. The overall roof was demolished in early 1992, and here we see one of the main beams being lowered to the ground on 1st May. Beyond the workmen, the shuttered bookstall is still standing against the south wall, but this building too will soon disappear. (D.C.Pearce)

109.   The whole atmosphere of the station changed after the roof was removed. With no shelter on the concourse or platforms, trains for Norwich and Ipswich wait at platforms 3 and 2 respectively on 28th February 1996. Fortunately this was a bright Winter day, but things could be very different with a gale blowing in from the nearby North Sea! (J.Sides)

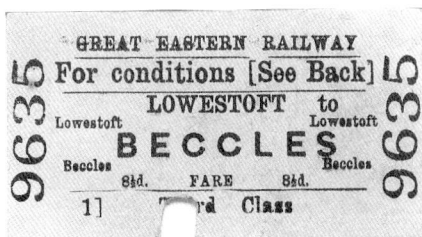

GREAT EASTERN RAILWAY
For conditions [See Back]
9635
LOWESTOFT   to
Lowestoft   Lowestoft
BECCLES
Beccles   Beccles
8½d.   FARE   8½d.
1]   rd   Class

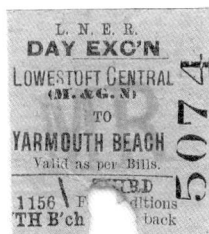

L. N. E. R.
DAY EXC'N
LOWESTOFT CENTRAL
(M. & G. N.)
TO
YARMOUTH BEACH
Valid as per Bills.
5074
1156   ditions
TH B'ch   back

5. Lowestoft Harbour Works & Harbour

LOWESTOFT HARBOUR WORKS

110.   As a major port, the town was subjected to bombing raids during World War II, and here we are looking down over the Harbour Works following one such attack. Our elevated viewpoint illustrates how the complex occupied a strip of land bordered by the waterfront and Commercial Road. In the middle distance, the substantial Iron Works, dating back to 1853, dominates a variety of smaller buildings around it. Over the years, this area served the railway in many ways, including the important task of looking after the vessels needed to maintain harbour operations, and it also incorporated a major concrete works between 1938 and 1985. (G.L.Kenworthy coll.)

➔   111. Two old GER wagons, one dating back to 1909 and the other to 1914, stand alongside Commercial Road during the 1950s. Emphasising the dockland environment, a lightship undergoes maintenance in the dry dock beyond, which was also owned by the railway authorities. After 118 years, the railway eventually relinquished control of the harbour from 1st January 1963, when the British Transport Docks Board took over responsibility. (NRS Archive)

112.   One day around 1960, Sentinel no. 38 was photographed within the confines of the Engineer's Depot. The curving track in front of it leads past the buildings on the north side of Commercial Road, across London Road and onto the fishwharf, before eventually making its way out to the eastern extremity of the British railway system. (NRS Archive)

113.   The street name identifies the location as we look at the east end of the complex on 19th February 1988. At this time the site was used to maintain track machines, and the line leading to the quayside had long been removed. The gate protecting this line is still there though, and behind it is a power unit for a viaduct inspection train, converted from a Grampus wagon during the 1960s. By now such oddities were becoming somewhat rare on an increasingly standardised railway network. Railway activity here ceased some two months later, and twenty years on, the buildings had been demolished and a supermarket occupied the site. (R.J.Adderson)

1919 Instruction, predating the use of tractors.

LOWESTOFT CENTRAL.

Horsing trucks across the Public Roads.

In moving a truck or trucks across the Public Roads at Lowestoft Central, named below, the Horse or Horses must not be attached to the side of the truck or trucks, **but must in all cases be attached in front,** so that persons passing along the Roads may see the whole operation.

(a) Station Crossing, London Road.

A competent man with a Red Flag by day and a Red Light by night is to be in attendance to warn the public in all cases when trucks are about to be moved across this Crossing.

(b) Harbour Yard Crossing, London Road.
(c) Belvedere Road Crossing, South Side.

At these crossings (b) and (c) the Horseman is to keep a sharp look out and warn the public in all cases when trucks are about to be moved across same.

The Station Master at Lowestoft Central must give his personal attention to see that these instructions are strictly carried out.

LOWESTOFT HARBOUR

XXII. What had begun as a "short harbour branch" of around ¼ mile in 1847 was extended over the following sixty years to ¾ mile in order to reach the eastern end of the North Pier around the docks constructed to accommodate the expansion of the fishing industry. The full extent is depicted on this 1950s plan at a scale of 12ins. to 1 mile. Rather than showing a chronological sequence, the photographs illustrate a journey from the London Road crossing immediately outside the station to the furthest extremity of the North Pier Extension.

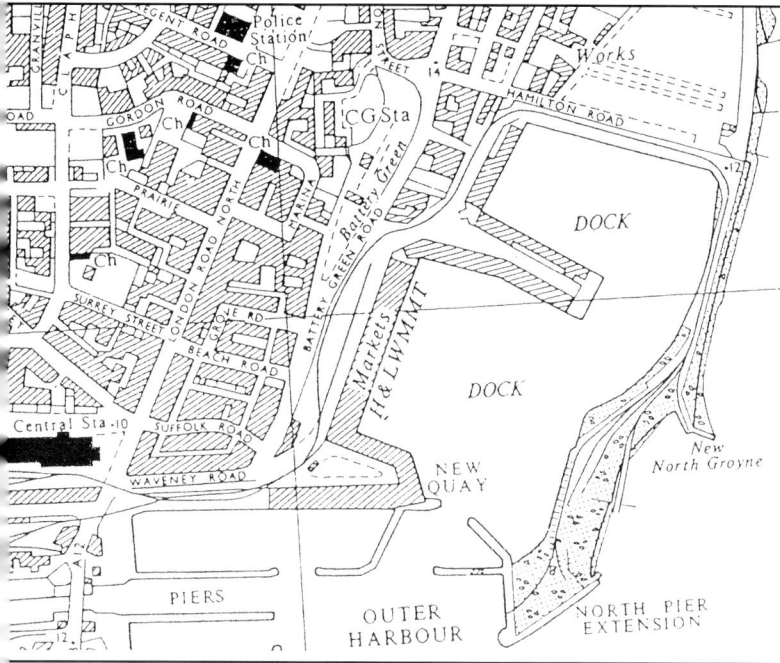

114. The line from the station shown in picture 105 crossed London Road a short distance to the north of the outlet from Commercial Road, a situation which led to some complex trackwork in the days when the town tramway system crossed these lines at right angles. A BR tractor brings road traffic to a standstill as it crosses the road with two wagons from the docks during the late 1960s. (G.H.Smith)

115.   We now cross London Road to take a look at the railways around the fish docks. In the first of four pictures taken on the same day, probably in the late 1950s, a Sentinel shunter makes its way along the north side of the Trawl Basin, with the buildings on Waveney Road beyond. (NRS Archive)

116.   Now we are looking eastwards, standing on the line from the Harbour Works, with the rails from the station coming in on the left. There are plenty of wagons on the quayside, and the trawler *Anguilla* is moored in the Trawl Basin. Although declining year by year, rail traffic from here lingered on until the early 1970s, by which time the fishing industry was a shadow of its former self. (NRS Archive)

117.   Our third picture features the complex trackwork half way along the Trawl Basin. A flagman is strolling along behind the train, as it takes the line which terminated out on the North Pier extension after running round three sides of the Waveney and Hamilton docks. These docks had been built by the GER in 1883 and 1906 respectively to cater for the rapidly expanding fishing industry. (NRS Archive)

Advertisement from 1912/3 GER timetable.

FISH DIRECT FROM THE MERCHANT. TO CONSUMER.

The following Reduced Rates are charged for conveyance of Parcels of Fish sent by Fish Merchants to Private Families by **PASSENGER TRAIN** from

YARMOUTH and LOWESTOFT to LONDON

and Stations on the Great Eastern Railway within 20 miles thereof, **including Delivery** within the usual Cartage limits.

Parcels not exceeding 16 lbs.   -   -   -   -   -   -   -   **4d.**
   ,,   over 16 lbs. and not exceeding 24 lbs.   -   -   -   -   **6d.**

These Rates are at Owner's Risk.

The following Merchants are sending out small Parcels of Fish direct to Consumers:—

YARMOUTH
Mr. BEAZOR, Nelson Road.
Mr. CHAPMAN, 39, Lichfield Road.
Mr. PARKER, Frog's Hall.
Mr. WILLIAM PYE, Vauxhall Curing Works, 53, North Quay.

Mr. F. E. SMITH, 4, Fish Market.
*Messrs. JOHN WOODGER & SONS. South Quay.
Mr. W. J. SMITH, North Sea Fish Stores, Gorleston.
THE REGENT FISH STORES, Regent Road.
* Dry Fish only.

LOWESTOFT
Mr. E. F. THAIN, Bridge Terrace.
Mr. B. MEWSE, High Street.
Mr. F. ARCHER, Suffolk Road.
Mr. G. GEARING. London Road South.

Mr. A. E. CREWS. London Road North.
Mr. E. WARTON, 135, Bevan Street.
Mr. H. HARRIS, 32, Stevens Street.

118.   Beyond Hamilton Dock, the line was used to transport another product of the North Sea. Continuous dredging was needed to keep the harbour entrance clear, a requirement that the railway was able to turn to its own advantage, both by using the material for internal purposes and selling it externally. We are standing at the north-eastern corner of Hamilton Dock, with the line curving slightly inland towards the tower of the distant shingle screening plant, which was part of the improvements effected by the LNER in 1938. This otherwise unremarkable stretch of track has the distinction of being the most easterly point on the British railway system. (NRS Archive)

119.   Out on the North Pier extension, a steam crane is busy excavating shingle from the seabed during the 1930s. It is standing on one of the two jetties which had been built for this purpose. (R.Shephard)

120.   This exposed stretch of railway was badly damaged by the storms and catastrophic flooding that affected much of the East Coast in February 1938. Here is the wrecked sea wall and part of the undermined track near to the north-eastern corner of Hamilton Dock a few days after the event. Unhindered by any Health and Safety legislation, the townspeople have flocked to the site to see the extent of the damage. The local newspaper reported that repair work went on for 18 hours a day, employing 150 men. They must have done their work well, for the railway here survived another battering in the 1953 floods, only to close in the late 1950s. (R.F.Bonny)

BEACH SHINGLE AND BEACH GRIT

from the EAST COAST.

These Materials can now be delivered at any Goods Station on the Great Eastern Railway, in Truck Loads, each containing 7 Tons or upwards, at a cost, including Carriage, *pro rata* to the mileage conveyed.
The Maximum Cost, including Carriage, is as under :—

	s. d.			s. d.	
No. 1. Beach Shingle	6 3 per Ton.	No. 4. Beach Grit (Fine for Asphalte) ...	7 9 per Ton.
„ 2. Beach Shingle (small)	7 0 „	„ 5. Beach Shingle (Fine for Asphalte)	7 9 „
„ 3. Beach Grit (Coarse for Asphalte) ... 7 3 „		„ 6. Beach Shingle (Extra Fine for Asphalte)	8 6 „

Full particulars can be obtained from, and orders should be addressed to the Goods Manager, Great Eastern Railway, Liverpool Street Station, London, E.C.,; or the District Goods Managers at Hamilton House, 183, Bishopsgate, London, E.C.; Norwich, Ipswich, and Cambridge.

SEA WATER BATHS.

Sea Water from Lowestoft is delivered daily, except Sundays and Bank Holidays, at any Station on the Railway, or at any address within the ordinary cartage delivery of the Company in **London, G.E. Suburban Stations,** and the Country, at one uniform price of **Sixpence** for every **Three Gallons,** payable on delivery. The Kegs containing the Water are perfectly tight, well corked, and fitted with a handle, to admit of their being easily carried upstairs ; they will be left by the Company's Carmen, if required for the convenience of the Consignee, and called for afterwards without extra charge.
The Company deliver in **London and G.E. Suburban Stations** in quantities of not less than **Twelve Gallons at Three Half-pence per Gallon.**
Orders may be sent by post, or given verbally to any Station Master on the Railway, or to the Carmen when delivering or collecting the Kegs, or to Mr. H. E. Smith, 179, Bishopsgate, E.C.

Advertisements from 1912/3 GER timetable.

MP Middleton Press

EVOLVING THE ULTIMATE RAIL ENCYCLOPEDIA

Easebourne Lane, Midhurst, West Sussex. GU29 9AZ Tel:01730 813169

www.middletonpress.co.uk email:info@middletonpress.co.uk

A-978 0 906520 B-978 1 873793 C-978 1 901706 D-978 1 904474 E-978 1 906008

OOP Out of print at time of printing - Please check availability BROCHURE AVAILABLE SHOWING NEW TITLES

A
Abergavenny to Merthyr C 91 8
Abertillery and Ebbw Vale Lines D 84 5
Aldgate & Stepney Tramways B 70 1
Allhallows - Branch Line to A 62 8
Alton - Branch Lines to A 11 6
Andover to Southampton A 82 6
Ascot - Branch Lines around A 64 2
Ashburton - Branch Line to B 95 4
Ashford - Steam to Eurostar B 67 1
Ashford to Dover A 48 2
Austrian Narrow Gauge D 04 3
Avonmouth - BL around D 42 5
Aylesbury to Rugby D 91 3
B
Baker Street to Uxbridge D 90 6
Banbury to Birmingham D 27 2
Barking to Southend C 80 2
Barnet & Finchley Tramways B 93 0
Barry - Branch Lines around D 50 0
Bath Green Park to Bristol C 36 9
Bath to Evercreech Junction A 60 4
Bath Tramways B 86 2
Battle over Portsmouth 1940 A 29 1
Battle over Sussex 1940 A 79 6
Bedford to Wellingborough D 31 9
Betwixt Petersfield & Midhurst A 94 9
Birmingham to Wolverhampton E 25 3
Birmingham Trolleybuses E 19 2
Blackpool Tramways 1933-66
Bletchley to Cambridge D 94 4
Bletchley to Rugby E 07 9
Blitz over Sussex 1941-42 B 35 0
Bodmin - Branch Lines around B 83 1
Bognor at War 1939-45 B 59 6
Bombers over Sussex 1943-45 B 51 0
Bournemouth & Poole Trys B 47 3
Bournemouth to Evercreech Jn A 46 8
Bournemouth to Weymouth A 57 4
Bournemouth Trolleybuses C 10 9
Bradford Trolleybuses D 19 7
Brecon to Neath D 43 2
Brecon to Newport D 16 6
Brecon to Newtown E 06 2
Brighton to Eastbourne A 16 1
Brighton to Worthing A 03 1
Brighton Trolleybuses D 34 0
Bristols Tramways B 57 2
Bristol to Taunton D 03 6
Bromley South to Rochester B 23 7
Bromsgrove to Birmingham D 87 6
Bromsgrove to Gloucester D 73 9
Brunel - A railtour of his achievements D 74 6
Bude - Branch Line to B 29 9
Burnham to Evercreech Jn A 68 0
Burton & Ashby Tramways C 51 2
C
Camberwell & West Norwood Tys B 22 0
Cambridge to Ely D 55 5
Canterbury - Branch Lines around B 58 9
Cardiff Trolleybuses D 64 7
Caterham & Tattenham Corner B 25 1
Changing Midhurst C 15 4
Chard and Yeovil - BLs around C 30 7
Charing Cross to Dartford A 75 8
Charing Cross to Orpington A 96 3
Cheddar - Branch Line to B 90 9
Cheltenham to Andover C 43 7
Cheltenham to Redditch D 81 4
Chesterfield Tramways D 37 1
Chesterfield Trolleybuses D 51 7
Chester Tramways E 04 8
Chichester to Portsmouth A 14 7
Clapham & Streatham Trys B 97 8
Clapham Junction to Beckenham Jn B 36 7
Cleobury Mortimer - BLs around E 18 5
Clevedon & Portishead - BLs to D 18 0
Collectors Trains, Trolleys & Trams D 29 6
Colonel Stephens D62 3
Cornwall Narrow Gauge D 56 2
Cowdray & Easebourne D 96 8
Craven Arms to Llandeilo E 35 2
Crawley to Littlehampton A 34 5
Cromer - Branch Lines around C 26 0
Croydons Tramways B 42 8
Croydons Trolleybuses B 73 2
Croydon to East Grinstead B 48 0
Crystal Palace (HL) & Catford Loop A 87 1
Cyprus Narrow Gauge E13 0
D
Darlington - Leamside - Newcastle E 28 4
Darlington to Newcastle D 98 2
Darlington Trolleybuses D 33 3
Dartford to Sittingbourne B 34 3
Derby Tramways D 17 3
Derby Trolleybuses C 72 7
Derwent Valley - Branch Line to the D 06 7
Devon Narrow Gauge E 09 3
Didcot to Banbury D 02 9
Didcot to Swindon C 84 0
Didcot to Winchester C 13 0
Dorset & Somerset Narrow Gauge D 76 0
Douglas to Peel C 88 8
Douglas to Port Erin C 55 0
Douglas to Ramsey D 39 5
Dovers Tramways B 24 4
Dover to Ramsgate A 78 9
Dublin Northwards in the 1950s
Dunstable - Branch Lines to E 27 7
E
Ealing to Slough C 42 0
East Cornwall Mineral Railways D 22 7
East Croydon to Three Bridges A 53 6
East Grinstead - Branch Lines to A 07 9
East Ham & West Ham Tramways B 52 7
East London - Branch Lines of C 44 4
East London Line B 80 0
East Ridings Secret Resistance D 21 0
Edgware & Willesden Tramways C 18 5
Effingham Junction - BLs around A 74 1
Ely to Norwich C 90 1
Embankment & Waterloo Tramways B 41 1
Enfield Town & Palace Gates - BL to D 32 6
Epsom to Horsham A 30 7
Eritrean Narrow Gauge E 38 3
Euston to Harrow & Wealdstone C 89 5
Exeter & Taunton Tramways B 32 9
Exeter to Barnstaple B 15 2
Exeter to Newton Abbot C 49 9
Exeter to Tavistock B 69 5
Exmouth - Branch Lines to B 00 8
F
Fairford - Branch Line to A 52 9
Falmouth, Helston & St. Ives - BL to C 74 1
Fareham to Salisbury A 67 3
Faversham to Dover B 05 3
Felixstowe & Aldeburgh - BL to D 20 3
Fenchurch Street to Barking C 20 8
Festiniog - 50 yrs of enterprise C 83 3
Festiniog 1946-55 E 01 7
Festiniog in the Fifties B 68 8
Festiniog in the Sixties B 91 6
Frome to Bristol B 77 0
Fulwell - Trams, Trolleys & Buses D 11 1
G
Gloucester to Bristol D 35 7
Gloucester to Cardiff D 66 1
Gosport & Horndean Trys B 92 3
Gosport - Branch Lines around A 36 9
Great Yarmouth Tramways D 13 5
Greece Narrow Gauge D 72 2
Grimsby & Cleethorpes Trolleybuses D 86 9
H
Hammersmith & Hounslow Trys C 33 8
Hampshire Narrow Gauge D 36 4
Hampstead & Highgate Tramways B 53 4
Harrow to Watford D 14 2
Hastings to Ashford A 37 6
Hastings Tramways B 18 3
Hawkhurst - Branch Line to A 66 6
Hay-on-Wye - Branch Lines around D 92 0
Hayling - Branch Line to A 12 3
Haywards Heath to Seaford A 28 4
Hemel Hempstead - Branch Lines to D 88 3
Henley, Windsor & Marlow - BL to C77 2
Hereford to Newport D 54 8
Hexham to Carlisle D 75 3
Hitchin to Peterborough D 07 4
Holborn & Finsbury Tramways B 79 4
Holborn Viaduct to Lewisham A 81 9
Horsham - Branch Lines to A 02 4
Huddersfield Tramways D 95 1
Huddersfield Trolleybuses C 92 5
Hull Tramways D60 9
Hull Trolleybuses D 24 1
Huntingdon - Branch Lines around A 93 2
I
Ilford & Barking Tramways B 61 9
Ilford to Shenfield C 97 0
Ilfracombe - Branch Line to B 21 3
Ilkeston & Glossop Tramways D 40 1
Index to Middleton Press Stations E 24 6
Industrial Rlys of the South East A 09 3
Ipswich to Saxmundham C 41 3
Ipswich Trolleybuses D 59 3
Isle of Wight Lines - 50 yrs C 12 3
K
Keighley Tramways & Trolleybuses D 83 8
Kent & East Sussex Waterways A 72 X
Kent Narrow Gauge C 45 1
Kent Seaways - Hoys to Hovercraft D 79 1
Kidderminster to Shrewsbury E10 9
Kingsbridge - Branch Line to C 98 7
Kingston & Hounslow Loops A 83 3
Kingston & Wimbledon Tramways B 56 5
Kingswear - Branch Line to C 17 8
L
Lambourn - Branch Line to C 70 3
Launceston & Princetown - BL to C 19 2
Lewisham to Dartford A 92 5
Lines around Wimbledon B 75 6
Liverpool Street to Chingford D 01 2
Liverpool Street to Ilford C 34 5
Liverpool Tramways - Eastern C 04 8
Liverpool Tramways - Northern C 46 8
Liverpool Tramways - Southern C 23 9
Llandudno & Colwyn Bay Tramways E 17 8
London Bridge to Addiscombe B 20 6
London Bridge to East Croydon A 58 1
London Termini - Past and Proposed D 00 5
London to Portsmouth Waterways B 43 5
Longmoor - Branch Lines to A 41 3
Looe - Branch Line to C 22 2
Lowestoft - Branch Lines around E 40 6
Ludlow to Hereford E 14 7
Lydney - Branch Lines around E 26 0
Lyme Regis - Branch Line to A 45 1
Lynton - Branch Line to B 04 6
M
Maidstone & Chatham Tramways B 40 4
March - Branch Lines around B 09 1
Margate & Ramsgate Tramways C 52 9
Marylebone to Rickmansworth D49 4
Melton Constable to Yarmouth Beach E 03 1
Mexborough to Swinton E 36 9
Midhurst - Branch Lines around A 49 9
Military Defence of West Sussex A 23 9
Military Signals, South Coast C 54 3
Minehead - Branch Line to A 80 2
Mitcham Junction Lines B 01 5
Mitchell & company C 59 8
Monmouth - Branch Lines to E 20 8
Monmouthshire Eastern Valleys D 71 5
Moreton-in-Marsh to Worcester D 26 5
Moretonhampstead - BL to C 27 7
Mountain Ash to Neath D 80 7
N
Newbury to Westbury C 66 6
Newcastle to Hexham D 69 2
Newcastle Trolleybuses D 78 4
Newport (IOW) - Branch Lines to A 26 0
Newquay - Branch Lines to C 71 0
Newton Abbot to Plymouth C 60 4
Northern France Narrow Gauge C 75 8
North East German Narrow Gauge D 44 9
North Kent Tramways B 44 2
North London Line B 94 7
North Woolwich - BLs around C 65 9
Norwich Tramways C 40 6
Nottinghamshire & Derbyshire T/B D 63 0
Nottinghamshire & Derbyshire T/W D 53 1
O
Ongar - Branch Lines to E 05 5
Oxford to Bletchley D57 9
Oxford to Moreton-in-Marsh D 15 9
P
Paddington to Ealing C 37 6
Paddington to Princes Risborough C 81 9
Padstow - Branch Line to B 54 1
Peterborough to Kings Lynn
Plymouth - BLs around B 98 5
Plymouth to St. Austell C 63 5
Pontypool to Mountain Ash D 65 4
Porthmadog 1954-94 - BL around B 31 2
Portmadoc 1923-46 - BL around B 13 8
Portsmouths Tramways B 72 5
Portsmouth to Southampton A 31 4
Potters Bar to Cambridge D 70 8
Princes Risborough - Branch Lines to D 05 0
Princes Risborough to Banbury C 85 7
R
Reading to Basingstoke B 27 5
Reading to Didcot C 79 6
Reading to Guildford A 47 5
Reading Tramways B 87 9
Reading Trolleybuses C 05 5
Redhill to Ashford A 73 4
Return to Blaenau 1970-82 C 64 2
Rickmansworth to Aylesbury D 61 6
Romania & Bulgaria Narrow Gauge E 23 9
Roman Roads of Hampshire D 67 8
Roman Roads of Kent E 02 4
Roman Roads of Surrey C 61 1
Roman Roads of Sussex C 48 2
Romneyrail C 32 1
Ross-on-Wye - Branch Lines around E 30 7
Rugby to Birmingham E 37 6
Ryde to Ventnor A 19 2
S
Salisbury to Westbury B 39 8
Saxmundham to Yarmouth C 69 7
Saxony Narrow Gauge D 47 0
Scarborough Tramways E 15 4
Seaton & Eastbourne Tramways B 76 3
Seaton & Sidmouth - Branch Lines to A 95 6
Secret Sussex Resistance B 82 4
Selsey - Branch Line to A 04 8
Shepherds Bush to Uxbridge T/Ws C 28 4
Shrewsbury - Branch Line to A 86 4
Shrewsbury to Ludlow E 21 5
Shrewsbury to Newtown E 29 1
Sierra Leone Narrow Gauge D 28 9
Sirhowy Valley Line E 12 3
Sittingbourne to Ramsgate A 90 1
Slough to Newbury C 56 7
Solent - Creeks, Crafts & Cargoes D 52 4
Southamptons Tramways B 33 6
Southampton to Bournemouth A 42 0
Southend-on-Sea Tramways B 28 2
Southern France Narrow Gauge C 47 5
Southwark & Deptford Tramways B 38 1
South W Harbours - Ships & Trades E 22 2
Southwold - Branch Line to A 15 4
South London Line B 46 6
South London Tramways 1903-33 D 10 4
South London Tramways 1933-52 D 89 0
South Shields Trolleybuses E 11 6
St. Albans to Bedford D 08 1
St. Austell to Penzance C 67 3
Stourbridge to Wolverhampton E 16 1
St. Pancras to Barking D 68 5
St. Pancras to St. Albans C 78 9
Stamford Hill Tramways B 85 5
Steaming through the Isle of Wight A 56 7
Steaming through West Hants A 69 7
Stratford upon Avon to Birmingham D 77 7
Stratford upon Avon to Cheltenham C 25 3
Surrey Home Guard C 57 4
Surrey Narrow Gauge C 87 1
Sussex Home Guard C 24 6
Sussex Narrow Gauge C 68 0
Swanley to Ashford B 45 9
Swindon to Bristol C 96 3
Swindon to Gloucester D46 3
Swindon to Newport D 30 2
Swiss Narrow Gauge C 94 9
T
Talyllyn - 50 years C 39 0
Taunton to Barnstaple B 60 2
Taunton to Exeter C 82 6
Tavistock to Plymouth B 88 6
Tees-side Trolleybuses D 58 6
Tenterden - Branch Line to A 21 5
Three Bridges to Brighton A 35 2
Tilbury Loop C 86 4
Tiverton - Branch Lines around C 62 8
Tivetshall to Beccles D 41 8
Tonbridge to Hastings A 44 4
Torrington - Branch Lines to B 37 4
Towcester - Branch Lines around E 39 0
Tunbridge Wells - Branch Lines to A 32 1
Twickenham & Kingston Trys C 35 2
U
Upwell - Branch Line to B 64 0
V
Victoria & Lambeth Tramways B 49 7
Victoria to Bromley South A 98 7
Vivarais Revisited E 08 6
W
Walthamstow & Leyton Tramways B 65 7
Waltham Cross & Edmonton Trys C 07 9
Wandsworth & Battersea Tramways B 63 3
Wantage - Branch Line to D 25 8
Wareham to Swanage - 50 yrs D 09 8
War on the Line A 10 9
Waterloo to Windsor A 54 3
Waterloo to Woking A 38 3
Watford to Leighton Buzzard D 45 6
Wenford Bridge to Fowey C 09 3
Westbury to Bath B 55 8
Westbury to Taunton C 76 5
West Cornwall Mineral Railways D 48 7
West Croydon to Epsom B 08 4
West German Narrow Gauge D 93 7
West London - Branch Lines of C 50 5
West London Line B 84 8
West Wiltshire - Branch Lines of D 12 8
Weymouth - Branch Lines around A 65 9
Willesden Junction to Richmond B 71 8
Wimbledon to Beckenham C 58 1
Wimbledon to Epsom B 62 6
Wimborne - Branch Lines around A 97 0
Wisbech - Branch Lines around C 01 7
Wisbech 1800-1901 C 93 2
Woking to Alton A 59 8
Woking to Portsmouth A 25 3
Woking to Southampton A 55 0
Wolverhampton Trolleybuses D 85 2
Woolwich & Dartford Trolleys B 66 4
Worcester to Birmingham D 97 5
Worcester to Hereford D 38 8
Worthing to Chichester A 06 2
Y
Yeovil - 50 yrs change C 38 3
Yeovil to Dorchester A 76 5
Yeovil to Exeter A 91 8
York Tramways & Trolleybuses D 82 1